ROARING PL▶YLIST
OF THOUGHTS

Using Music to Release your Lioness and
Chase Away the Butterflies

ELOISA DAVIS

BALBOA.
PRESS
A DIVISION OF HAY HOUSE

Balboa Press books may be ordered through booksellers or by contacting:

Balboa Press
A Division of Hay House
1663 Liberty Drive
Bloomington, IN 47403
www.balboapress.co.uk
1 (877) 407-4847

Because of the dynamic nature of the Internet, any web addresses or links contained in this book may have changed since publication and may no longer be valid. The views expressed in this work are solely those of the author and do not necessarily reflect the views of the publisher, and the publisher hereby disclaims any responsibility for them.

The author of this book does not dispense medical advice or prescribe the use of any technique as a form of treatment for physical, emotional, or medical problems without the advice of a physician, either directly or indirectly. The intent of the author is only to offer information of a general nature to help you in your quest for emotional and spiritual well-being. In the event you use any of the information in this book for yourself, which is your constitutional right, the author and the publisher assume no responsibility for your actions.

Any people depicted in stock imagery provided by Getty Images are models, and such images are being used for illustrative purposes only. Certain stock imagery © Getty Images.

Print information available on the last page.

ISBN: 978-1-9822-8077-2 (sc)
ISBN: 978-1-9822-8079-6 (hc)
ISBN: 978-1-9822-8078-9 (e)

Balboa Press rev. date: 06/18/2019

CONTENTS

This book is dedicated to:

Saying 'no'. Our mothers. Our sisters. Our spirit sisters. Our daughters. Our cousins. Our grandmothers. Our best friends. Girls. Women. You. The future.

ACKNOWLEDGEMENTS

To my Grandad Opa for inspiring this novel to be magical and for our connection. This adventure helped me get back to who I really was, the 'Sunshine Girl'. Thank you to my wonderful publishers for believing in my story. Thank you to my lovely editor Kirsten for your support and guidance.

Thank you to all the beautiful artists mentioned in this book, your music was my real medicine. Thank you also to my real life artists who are mentioned in this book.

To my whole book family and everyone who has supported this message, you have made those bad dreams seem like a different life. Reality now feels like a sunshine parallel world. Gratitude to you all at Balboa Press and Hay House for shining a light on my life. And finally, to the women I met at Hay House and Louise Hay herself for inspiring me to shine my light.

A SPRINKLE OF 'MAGIC': REVEALING 'HOW' THIS BOOK CAME ABOUT

Why did you choose *this* novel?
Was it the *picture*?
The *font*?
The *colour* scheme?
The *words* in the title?

I have a feeling it is so much more than that. It may have been the word 'music' or the idea of 'chasing away butterflies'. It could have been the word 'lioness' that caught your eye. Whatever it was that caught your sparkly eye, own it. This is your magical adventure. Mine and yours. *You and I.* We will be singing and dancing as we skip and groove through these pages. We will begin this journey as lion cubs, ending in brave lionesses. We will be exploring why and how the development will happen later in the novel - together as lionesses.

Everything happens in life at the exact right time. I never knew this until I started writing this book. This adventure will go through a series of playlists: musical playlists. These are songs I have listened to in my life. Although you girl, will be choosing your own. Whatever you are blaring through those lovely headphones is there for a reason. You are 'tapped in, tuned in, turned on' (Abraham Hicks). It has meaning for you. It makes you who you are. Remember that.

In this magical adventure, we will be listening and dancing through a series of playlists. I encourage you to feel a good 'vibe' through the lyrics from the magnificent Beyoncé, the honest 'Ed Sheeran', the powerful 'Little Mix', the beautiful 'Ariana Grande', the inspirationally independent genius that is Stevie Wonder, the royal Ella Eyre, Loud Luxury, ChainSmokers, and various R'n'B references with a sprinkle of hip hop.

I will be discussing my own experiences and lessons so you can relate these to your life. I will discuss my experiences but as the reader, it is your role to think of your own life when I speak about mine. In reading this book, you will learn that if you apply confidence and self-belief the way I do then ultimately you will feel brave enough to avoid situations or experiences that may make you feel less good and help prevent unnecessary pain.

I had my first panic attack at sixteen and I could never really make sense of it or why it happened. This developed into illnesses over a six-year period. I first had a particular experience in 'Hey House', my house in the halls at university, something I always saw as a 'mistake' has since been magically transformed into a 'blessing'.

This is something I believe is thanks to Rhonda Byrne who wrote 'The Secret'. It has added a sense of 'realism' to this journey of how to feel good about your past, present, and future. I started this journey of self-discovery as an unconfident girl, always just trying to be 'brave' and 'happy'. I created a somewhat 'pretend smile' displayed to the world which didn't reflect how I truly felt. After finishing this novel, I have become not only a woman but so much more. I am now writing this as a strong, confident woman bursting with joy. After finishing this novel, I have become not only a woman but so much more. This is purely coming from a girl who was scared to be a woman and the lovely 'sunshine girl' that her family and friends knew and loved has strongly returned. With a roar.

Honesty and a sprinkle of 'self-love' join us on this journey. I want you to get as much from this adventure as I have. The only way for this to happen is to believe in yourself and to remember who you are.

I am inspired by novels I have only been able to understand and read in the past few months because of previous beliefs and the uncertainty of the world's intentions for me. I now know who I am and that is why I am ready to tell you and share my experiences to give you the gift I have received. No matter the darkness, there are still stars. I promise. Let us shine a light on the past.

'Dare to love yourself as if you were a rainbow with gold at both ends' - Aberjhani - from 'Believe in yourself you are amazing' (Summersdale Publishers Ltd).

I want this book to stay with you. I want it to give you hope and for you to believe in the words of Audrey Hepburn, 'Nothing is impossible. The word itself says I'm possible!' That is you.

This magical adventure has been given to you at the perfect point of your life as a girl, in reality, a woman. Relate this 'Roaring Playlist' to your life today.

You are beautiful. I know I am. I never knew this before I started writing in Louis Armstrong's gorgeous words, 'the wonderful world'. Thank you, Louis. Yes, I do now see 'trees of green, red roses too, I see them bloom for me and you and I think to myself what a wonderful world!' This song that was played at my Grandad's funeral. A heartbreak turned into a heart-up thanks to this adventure. Sending you a huge virtual, sunshine hug.

E. x

P.S. I have a feeling you too will start to see your 'true colours shining through'. Thank you, Fredro Starr. I always loved the film 'Save The Last dance'. It makes me want to dance. I aim to help you groove through this adventure.

Let's paint that magical canvas together. Only if you want or believe you will get this from reading these words.

I never say 'goodbye', it feels too final. See ya, girl!

INTRODUCTION

Hello you. Hello, you beautiful thing. I mean I 'kinda' want to begin this with some kind of song. A tune that you, my friend chooses. One song. Your absolute favourite beat out there. You thought of one, didn't you!? If you didn't, I believe you will. It may be related to something, someone, or even a place. Take yourself there to that place. Don't think about it, just do it. Think of that special person or place that instantly makes your face itch and twitch with a smile.

It may be a special someone, a friend, a best friend who could be anywhere in the world right now. As far as Melbourne to England. It may be a special relative or even a boyfriend. Or a place. That hot destination you have only ever seen in your sparkling dreams. You have the image now, don't you? I hope so.

Right, now when you think of that person who has possibly impacted your life, what song comes to mind? The genre may be romance. It might be comedy. It could be adventure. Whatever it is, visualise the song through singing anything that comes to mind now that you have that place, person, or object in your imagination.

My aim of this book is to connect with you. Create sparkling endorphins and encourage you as the brave, unique, kind, inspiring lioness that is in you, bursting to reveal herself, to believe in yourself, and to experience through these pages, the magical adventure that is eagerly waiting at the 'Arrivals Lounge' at your closest destination. My aim will be for us both to start looking at our thoughts as a playlist. Let's choose the ones we love!

I have a question for you, my friend. Do you want to feel good now? Not in the future. Now. If the answer is yes, then this book has been hand delivered to you for that very reason. I truly believe there is a reason you were drawn to this book. I cannot thank you enough for this choice.

Remember Nala from the 'Lion King' The lovely little cub. I loved the film and how she blossoms in the story. She radiates sunshine and is so brave. Tiny lionesses roar the absolute loudest, and that my friend is you. (Thank you to Pennyhill Park Spa in Bagshot for inspiring this, your stain glass window caught my eye).

In real life, we often forget the dazzling love and journey that can exist when you believe in yourself. It results in reaching that 'self-love' destination. Do you want to catch that first-class ticket to your desired destination? Carry on reading and you will witness, but more importantly, *experience* the journey to your desired beautiful destination.

Quick, your transport is approaching! What are we doing? I'm jumping on! Are you? Great, see you onboard. I'll be the girl sitting in that coach, probably sipping on a hazelnut latte. I have never believed so much in something before, girl. Welcome to the jungle, you gorgeous thing.

GRATITUDE

As we go on this adventure together I am going to be doing it with you. Every single step. Every moment, every practice, every feeling I am going to be there every step of the way.

Why? Your creative mind may be thinking. The reason is I want to experience this with you. Any questions you have I want to be able to connect with you. Not as a doctor. Not as a teacher. Not as a therapist. As a fellow lioness. I want to hear you roar! We will roar together.

I cannot begin this without gratitude. Gratitude is the foundation of these pages. Without gratitude, this book does not exist.

This sunshine adventure has been delivered to the world through the incredible belief and hard work from my beautiful publishers and lovely editor. Gratitude feels like an understatement for my book family. Thank you so much to Balboa Press for believing in me and this story. Thank you to my kind editor for your support and guidance to make this journey even more special. With the contributed love and support you have both given me, this book has become a magical reality. I cannot thank you enough. Thank you for believing in the sunshine adventure, believing in me and the sparkly future for women. I never dreamed that my book would be published in the Hay House catalogue so my own reality is better than those uncertain dreams now.

So, here it is. The first practice. Who are we thanking girl? It may be a family member. Ah okay. Here's mine. My loving parents. Firstly, their endless support and belief in the lioness. The girl they knew was there, bursting to jump out and roar.

It may be that angel in a form of a best friend. The one you all your 'bestie'. The lemonade to your lemons. The one you are convinced has angel wings. Yes, her or him! Let's thank them. My best friend is an absolute angel. Thank you for being my secret sister. Thank you to all my friends, you are honestly all ace and you make me who I am today.

I have a feeling there is a sibling or a close relative who you think the sun pretty much shines out of their...yes, them! Let's thank them. Thank you to my brother for being my rock. You inspire me on a daily basis.

Ah, another one! One more maybe. This feels good, doesn't it! Feeling a little euphoric? It's amazing how good a bit of 'taa' (thank you) can do for your well-being. I've got mine! Have you got yours? I have two people. I got a little carried away. These are the ones we connect with on another level. You may not see them as much as you would like to but you know they are there. Spiritually? For me, correct. For you, it may be emotionally or even physically. You can't explain or describe it. Think of 'sisterhood' or your girl/boy 'squad'. Voila!

Right. Then we have the last but definitely not least. The lion. The one who never fails to put a smile on your face. This is an interesting one, he/she may be in your life or they may not be. It makes this adventure that little bit more exciting, right?! I believe by the end of this book that strong, inspiring, kind, brave lioness will reveal more about this. Not by speaking a direct name no, our heart will beat to the 'Simba' we would like.

Ready, my lioness? You were born ready. Be yourself when you read this and my gosh, if I can guarantee anything from these pages it is feelings of gratitude, appreciation, and self-love of everything around you - including yourself. Something I have been practising every day since reading Rhonda Byrne's book 'The Secret'. Gratitude moving us into the paw prints of self-belief. The most rewarding part of self - discovery. All yours. Now, let the magical adventure commence. Woohoo! Self-love, 'where you at?' We are ready for you. Roar.

PL ▶ YLIST

THE BIRTH OF THE CUB

Hello Princess Lioness, you brave thing.

'You are braver than you believe, stronger than you seem, and smarter than you think.' - A.A. Milne. (Summerdales Publishers Ltd).

Who is in charge of their bodies and mind ...what we thinking girl(s)?

What words, thoughts, and visual images are we having? I have a feeling we will have similar ideas. I'm not sure why, I simply cannot answer that. It could be this inner feeling and connection we are both receiving from something that is uniting us. I want to say the magical vibrations of the Universe, but I have this feeling your explanation is a lot *braver, stronger, and smarter* than you ever even realised.

I'll start. Name: Beyoncé. Were you thinking the same? I bet you were. Is it because this woman is an epitome of a strong, powerful woman? I agree. Words? Initially, I am thinking physically she is strong, inspirational, and natural. Three words! I feel as though my words are quite simple but for the moment I am sticking with this. I believe this to be very true and I feel a bit warm and futuristic now when I think of Beyoncé. A warmth relating to her wholesome, heartwarming personality and futuristic correlating with her mind. This is my initial thought, I believe *yours* is much more inspiring.

When you think the words, take your time and do this slowly.

Feel each word, believe each word as you envision them. My gosh. I did this and I feel as though she is right there. It is amazing what a bit of visualisation can do, isn't it?

Pop your left hand on your heart. Yeah sounds a bit different, I'm going to say 'quirky' but I can assure you, 'though this be madness, yet there is method in it.' Thank you, William Shakespeare! Now take that lovely, soft, right hand attached to your right arm. Pop it on your head. Feel that warmth. Woah. Wait. Pretty sure I just referred to you as having soft, lovely attributes that are creating warmth. Similar to the one and only, Beyoncé.

I am not sure why I said that, who knows. I felt it and now very much believe this is because of you. When this exercise happened for me, I could see Beyoncé in my mind even more. I even closed my eyes. Could you? I hope so. Either way, I think this confirms we are here for a reason and you, as the reader are creating this experience. Not me. Not the practice. You. You, my friend, are feeling this. This feels good doesn't it? I am not sure about you, but I am smiling right now. I think and believe the gorgeous little cub was born and opened her almond shape eyelids for the first time. Did you know 'Nala' means 'gift' in Swahili. Thank you, Wikipedia! Interesting eh?! We will definitely be coming back to this little phrase later.

So, the explanation for this seemingly 'quirky' exercise is because of the link between that wonderful heart of yours and that highly intelligent brain you have. The sources of so much feeling and thinking. Didn't think they were linked? Before the 27th January 2019, neither did I girl. Or maybe you actually did. You probably did know this but never realised. See! You are not only inspiring me, you are inspiring yourself. This is something I learned when I visited Harry Edwards Healing Sanctuary in Shere and met with and spoke to a lovely healer.

As we approach the end of this initial imagery are you thinking or feeling anything else? Make a note. I'm going with *radiant*. I'm not sure why. I'm sure there is a reason. I see a huge amount of sunshine in her. I believe she radiates a light where she goes. So, for now let us practice some more gratitude. Whether it be for your sparkly, dazzling eyes that allow you to see the picture or visual image of Beyoncé. Thank you, eyes! It may be feelings of gratitude for the words you personally were drawn to. Let's thank your creative mind. Thank you for *our* inspiring, magical minds. You may have more feelings of gratitude for other organs or lovely attributes of yours that have aided your visualisation. Let's give them a big, warm virtual hug and thanks.

How did it feel to thank what we have thanked? This is all you. Your thoughts, feelings, and thus reward. The reward being thankful and grateful for what you have. Own it girl. Your feelings are starting to have a bit more warmth and sort of 'lightness' right? Fabulous. Let's continue. The image you saw in your mind of Beyoncé is you as a young lioness cub. A bit like when Beyoncé was in Destiny's Child with her gorgeous girl squad Michelle and Kelly. What a dream team of lionesses.

Welcome to the world Baey, you gorgeous little cub. P.S. you are looking rather natural right now! What's your secret? I can't wait to find out and to be inspired even more. I have this feeling it is going to make me want to share with the stunning worldwide audience that is looking at you in absolute awe, this secret radiance that you have kept quiet all these years. Intentionally, absolutely not. It is happening now, we are feeling good now. Your future thoughts and feelings are happening now. You are shaping who you want to be as we connect now.

My gorgeous lioness cub. During this chapter, I am going to call you Baey. I hope and believe this is the perfect name for you right now. Baey because of Bae and I threw in a letter to make it appear as though it is like the stunning Queen herself. If we can imagine it, then we can visualise it. The idea of you as Beyoncé will very much be the focus of this chapter. The whole book your creative mind is thinking? No, it won't be. I think you and I both know we are going to explore thoughts, feelings and exercises not just as that lovely, unique little cub that has just been born but as so much more my friend. Why? I just believe it. I have never believed in something so sacred, so lovely and my gosh so naturally in my life. The reason being that you are not only portraying self-belief, you are beginning your magical journey of self-discovery equating to self-love.

So, Beyoncé is our dominant focus in this chapter. I am currently listening to the song 'Who run the world (girls)'. I would absolutely love if you did the same so we can feel, think, and believe every lyric together. If you do not have access to it right now, do you know what

Baey? That is more than fine. That is g.r.e.a.t. I can share them with you. Team Lionesses! Conquering this incredible adventure, paw by paw...*together.*

The lyrics of this song are really something. Okay, so initially when I turn the song on I have to admit I get a little shiver. The harmony? The pace? The tone? The rhythm? Yeah, yep...YES!! I'm going to go as far as saying these lyrics and the opening make me feel warm and calm. Until the beat hits then I think and feel as though I can do anything with my life. Do you agree? I'll give you a little clue as to why if you do not have access to the song. I mean I won't lie, even the words 'Who run the world?' make me physically and mentally spring off my seat. That kind of thought you have when you see a strong woman singing or doing something incredible and you can't help but clap, in reality or in your mind equally are empowering for both that person and yourself. 'My persuasion can build a nation. Endless power, with our love we can devour'. Beyoncé we are definitely persuaded, right Baey?

Girl. These lyrics, I feel as though they are for us. The previous generations who worked to get us here, our generation, and the next generation. This beautiful song has initially been a thought, where Beyoncé believed in it. If we believe these lyrics which I know you do, we can conquer. I think we can conclude that we believe they are true. Manifestation happened. 'To the other men that respect what I do please accept my shine'. I just shivered again. Beyoncé wanted to share with the world what she believed in. I have never realised that until now. Now, when we connected. You and I. You are bringing me so much inspiration I don't think you realise. So for this incredible revelation, I thank you Baey. Thank YOU for choosing this book, reading these words. It is through you that this is happening. The young little lioness cub who is revealing her princess nature that if I'm honest I never really appreciated so much until these words hit the paper. *Our connection.* My aim of this sunshine adventure is to help you see that you are a queen, exactly as you are. There are lionesses in the jungle, then there is you. That is your power. Beyoncé has helped us remind ourselves of this right?

Seeing as a truly honest personal interpretation of Beyoncé's music has strengthened our connection, I vow to be as honest as I can be in this book. Why? The sole reason I want us to connect so you can see that magic and love does exist, we just want a bit of self-love sprinkled all over us right?

Baey. How are you feeling right now? I don't like asking in terms of a 'scale'. To be honest I am not a massive fan of scales. Haha. Scale, scales, see what I did there? I don't think how we deeply, truly feel can be reflected in a number. So I am going to ask you to think of a word. Think of that word that instantly came to that incredible mind of yours. It may be happy. It may be loving. It may be excitement. Notice that I am using only positive words. My aim is for you and I both to have solely, good, positive feelings and thoughts. The reason for this is because much of what you think affects how you feel. Especially about yourself. You probably knew that anyway didn't you, my lovely little cub!

So let's focus on that word you instantly thought of, the one that came quick to you. We're talking 'Usain Bolt' quick. I'll start. I am feeling happy. Do I always feel happy? I am going to say until I began this adventure with you, Baey, nope I haven't. Then we connected and as this journey has started I have been pretty happy, ecstatic in fact. Why? I have thought positively which then has affected how I feel. It really is as simple as that. I will go into this through the book. Although, I think and therefore feel as though you began to notice this when we did that first practice with the hand on your head and the other on your heart. I bet you realised this before me Baey, of course you did you creative genius!

Okay, so right now I am feeling happy. I am actually smiling quite a lot right now. I want you to think of something that makes you happy. It may be a person, a relative. or a place. It may even be your favourite chocolate bar. I do love a Yorkie bar. If you feed me one of those I can guarantee a very big smile. The reason for this exercise Baey is because I want you to smile. If you smile I can assure you, the world will smile with you. One positive thought...will attract more positive thoughts, feelings, people, events, and experiences. We want to feel good now right now, yeah? No matter where you are, give us all a smile girl and I promise you this, I am smiling too. With you. With the world. Allow yourself some 'Love on Top'. Thank you, Beyoncé!

Right, now that we are smiling. I'd love to share with you why it was Beyoncé who I likened you to. The main reason being that I sense you are brave. Why? You chose this book. That in itself is brave. I believe you were drawn to the words of maybe 'chasing away butterflies' or this concept of becoming a lioness which further shows your brave inner self and being. Am I right? Or maybe it was the idea of seeing your mind as a magical playlist where you have already realised that music can be used to release an inner 'roar'. Learning about yourself and your mind could be seen to be a little daunting, but girl you grabbed the opportunity. For that you are courageous. If I have learnt anything in this book so far, it is that self-discovery and self-belief will get you well on the way to that beautiful destination you are seeking to reach. Once you know yourself fully I believe Baey, that you will conquer. Just like Beyoncé has.

The similarities I see between you both girl are here. Staring me in the face. Can you think of a time you were brave? It could literally be anything. Big or small. It may be when you applied to that school you didn't think you would get into. Perhaps when you asked your mum if you could borrow change for that chocolate bar you so desperately wanted to get your teeth into. Yet for you Baey, I think and believe you have done something a little braver. Let's think of that brave moment. As we started talking I said I would be honest, as honest I could be, here goes...my brave moment.

Around Christmas time, I had two weeks off work for stress. Why? You may be asking. The sole reason being stress. Wow, I've said it twice now. It's something I am not going to focus on because Baey that is the opposite of what I want for you. I want to focus on the absolute good for you. I want to be brave, strong for you. I believe that through speaking positively we are going to reach that destination of self-love. I think both of us are starting to see in the distance. Hello self-love, we are coming for you! I knew when I started writing this adventure I had found happiness, happiness with you and through your bravery of choosing a book on self-discovery, I feel it.

The reason I am focusing on bravery so much is because it is the foundation of learning about yourself. If you are brave, you will ask questions. You will make choices in your life mindfully. You speak a voice of what you believe and want. My bravery has been handing my notice into work. Why you ask? How? I did this solely to be happy Baey.

I have found what makes me happy. It is writing. Writing to that young, talented individual, you who is beginning their journey of self-discovery. I believe it to be brave. It is an incredible job I left but I know my happy face is there when I write to you. I want you to think of that brave moment you had earlier. Big or small. I went big because I want to feel brave. Yes, I may be a bit older than you, eek. Even if I'm not, there are no expectations on big or small. If yours is huge to you then it is braver than mine already! I want to reach full self-belief with you so we can laugh and roar together. We have achieved step one, bravery. Tick.

Think of that brave moment you have had. I hope you feel brave when you think of it Baey. Feel it. Maybe say it a few times to remind yourself of how brave you really are. You could even say the word 'brave' and do that lovely smile of yours that infects so wonderfully to the world. When you feel good and smile you attract more of it into your life. You are brave and I bet your face lights up even more when you smile. Let's give thanks Baey, great thanks for being incredibly brave, strong and for creating such a lovely dazzling smile.

If I'm honest girl I love all of Beyoncé's songs. Is it the same for you? My first ever concert was seeing the inspirational Destiny's Child and to be honest that is one of the main special moments I look back on and see real hope in terms of a future. Songs such as 'Independent Women' and 'Survivor' are songs I still play today. Yes. On repeat. 'Independent Women' is a song that my brother first introduced me to when we used to dance and sing together as young cubs.

I have a vivid image of him popping his head up saying, 'Question?' I would burst out laughing and probably dance or clap in response to this. Little did I know then he was actually teaching me to be independent. Furthermore, the song 'Survivor' has inspired very much a lot of this adventure. I heard it recently and I thought 'Bingo!' There it is. The song that has made me who I am. To be honest I find the whole song an inspiration but I will leave a few lyrics with you as I end this playlist. 'I'm a survivor (what), I'm not gon' give up (what) I'm not gon' stop (what), I'm gon' work harder (what) I'm a survivor (what), I'm gonna make it (what) I will survive (what), keep on survivin' (what).' That survivor is you my friend.

I am going to mention a song of Beyoncé's which I honestly adore. 'Hold up'. I saw the video of this and I'm pretty sure I clapped when I saw it. Whether or not this was in my mind or not I can't be certain! Either way I found it extremely powerful and inspiring. When I fell ill back when I was twenty-one years old with psychosis I did not feel myself for years Baey. Years. However, I returned when I started writing to you.

The other day I thought of a word that made me smile, 'Psych. No.Sis.' Psychosis with a quirky little touch up - the word 'no', something I hope you feel you can always say if you do not want to do something. 'What's worse, lookin' jealous or crazy? Jealous or crazy? Or like being walked all over lately, walked all over lately I'd rather be crazy'. I'll just leave that one with you, Sister. I know what I would rather be now. Thank you Beyoncé for shining a light on previous thoughts of seeing 'crazy' as something shameful. You are ace.

Girl, thank you for being brave. I hope you continue to see your bravery through that eye-catching smile of yours. I will see ya in the next chapter. 'She believed she could, so she did' (Paperchase Postcard). Yes Baey, you bloody well did. Without even realising, I believe fully until now. I have just put 'Perfect duet' on by Beyoncé and Ed Sheeran. I never thought there was something 'perfect' until I started writing. We are perfect. We are loved. We are enough, exactly as we are. Perfect is exactly how you imagine it. You. We are all a little bit of perfect. My mum called me 'imperfectly perfect' once and I thought it was a magical way to see this concept of perfection.

For now, it is see ya. Tiny lionesses roar the loudest my friend and your brave nature is revealing itself. Let's give thanks to that brave, courageous strength of yours. I think and feel, believe such bravery will be shown even more in the magical life that you are starting to see. It has always been there but I imagine you will start to see even more situations supporting this. See ya in the next chapter girl!

Looking forward to it.

E. x

P.S. Remember the song 'Best thing I never had' - Beyoncé. A song which my best friend sent me that I am convinced cured a break up. Thank you to Beyoncé and thank you to the angel I get to call my bestie. Music really can be therapy Princess.

Putting Playlist 1 Into Practice

Bravery. Strength. Smart. The idea of using 'your brain'.

By realising the link between your mind and your heart, you will gain an in-depth understanding. What you are thinking can affect how you feel. It may sound simple but before I knew they were connected I used to think and act quite 'robotically'. I felt as though I was living a life quite mechanically in which I acted in ways that I thought would be more practical. I felt things but would find it hard to express honestly what I meant.

Connecting your heart and your brain means that you can actively choose positive thoughts, which in turn will affect how you feel about things giving you positive experiences. For example, next time you want a positive outcome such as when you are going for a job interview or applying for a course, think about the person or experience in a positive way and imagine happening. You are more likely to get results that make you feel good if you approach it with positive thinking.

My mum often says, "We are human beings Ells, not doings". The first practise of gratitude: the reason for using gratitude is simple. I learnt it in 'The Secret' - if we feel grateful for what we have - even small things, they actually do come back to us multiplied - for example thanking a song, thanking a family member, thanking food means all of these experiences become richer and we attract more moments of this nature. A feel good vibe approach to life. Try it today!

My initial analysis of Beyoncé's lyrics - the songs we listen to have been written for a reason. People do not just write lyrics, they experience something and they want to share the positivity it has with other people. Even just simply the title, 'Who run the world (girls)' shows that there are infinite possibilities for you to think positively about your past, present, and future.

Thinking of your feelings as words as opposed to a scale steps away from seeing yourself as a number. Often people going through something are treated as though they are a number but adding a word can make you feel as though whatever you are thinking is unique to you.

Main teaching: Thinking positively affects how you feel not only about the world but yourself too. Positive self talk is so important. Also, the theme of this chapter is bravery - women in today's world have a voice. We are able to now speak about what we want and have the opportunity to do something and have experiences that we desire. Yet, I do feel some women (my past self included) do not have this voice. I felt scared to be a real woman in today's world and say 'no' to experiences because I was worried what people would think or if I had the 'right'. I was a people pleaser, putting others before myself, and I never felt good because it wasn't for me. I want you to come away feeling that you can say 'no' and actually it is very brave also extremely empowering to do so.

Share what you told yourself today on Instagram using #TheSunshineAdventure @eloisaroars If you want you can even use this to stay accountable to positivity and do this weekly!

PL▶YLIST 2

'MULTIPLY YOUR OPENNESS'

Hello Ed, you honest thing.

'Every day brings a chance for you to draw in a breath, kick off your shoes...and dance'. - Oprah Winfrey.

Girl. It's only been a page and I've missed you! Let's begin. I have this sparkly feeling that this is going to be a fun-filled playlist. Why, you inquisitive bubble of loveliness may be asking. The sole reason being my aim of this chapter is to make us both get a little twitch in those wonderful feet that our lovely bodies are attached to. Twitch? Eh?! Yes. I want us to be dancing and in the life-changing words of Ed Sheeran, I want you to 'Sing!'

You may have noticed that I have been using lyrics, musical lyrics in these pages so far. I am a music fan yes girl. I have a feeling you may be too and if you aren't a music fan I want to share with you the lyrics that have made me who I am and why I think music is the source of not just inspiration but it is the songs we choose, the lyrics we listen to that can affect how we feel. We would never choose a song we didn't want to listen to would we, girl? I actually see music as a form of therapy. I never knew this until I started this magical adventure with you.

I find Ed's lyrics SO honest as in they are very real and I think he touches on subjects that in the past may have not been accepted - he is accountable because he talks about his honest experiences. The 'Bloodstream' lyrics I have listened to so times and I'm pretty sure it is about him taking drugs. I could be wrong but I feel Ed is honest in his lyrics which really benefits his listeners so we can relate to him. Honesty similarly has got me to recovery hence why his music was my daily medicine in hospital and for years after.

I am going to make a small reference to the previous chapter. I hope you don't mind. The reason being I want the chapters to flow. There has been no pre-planned structure. Yes, I have thought of themes but the structure has come I first thought of connecting with you. Every word is written with you in mind, girl. Young woman, the reason for this is I am experiencing this with you. Every millisecond. I want it to be real and honest. I want to be open with you and continue this throughout. In the words of Neyo and Calvin Harris in their song 'Let's Go', "It's not about what you've done it's about what you doing. It's all about where you going no matter where you've been.... Let's go!"

Around the time I was working on this chapter, I went back to the incredible company who gave me an award at Christmas for the 'Best Newcomer'. They called the award the Eloisa 'Ray of Sunshine' Davis award. My parents called me 'Sunshine Girl' when I was young and I never felt it until I started my passion. Writing to you. The young women of this wonderful world. I now see that young girl. They always knew she was there but hiding behind a mind of self-doubt and a tiny voice. This is my link to feeling happy girl, writing to you.

Even so, I knew the job itself wasn't right for me. So I walked into the office one day with my resignation letter. I handed it to our kind director who always believed in me. I cried like I haven't cried in years. Crying with feeling and emotion. A really good kind of 'cry'. I was sent home. Sent home from the best job I have ever had. Why, you're probably asking? I was not as happy as I am now, girl.

The company has given me incredible confidence but my 'sunshine' heart is in writing. For the first time (ever!) I have been truly honest with not only a company but to myself. Myself being the most important part. If I am happy, which I am now...everything has started to fall into place. It all makes a bit more 'sense'. I very much believe this to be true. I am telling you this because I want the same for you. I want you to dance and sing through this chapter. Not for me, not for anyone else but for *you*. I think honesty is such a powerful concept.

If you are honest with yourself then ask yourself if you truly are okay. If what you are doing or thinking at that exact moment is truly contributing to your happy feelings. If it is that is incredible. If not, it is my aim to help you get there to freely *choose* the experiences you want to have. The openness you expose yourself to when you are honest with what you want out of life is so powerful, girl. It is magical. I can't wait to continue this musical adventure with you. Paw by paw. Together.

So let's begin. Who is your ultimate favourite artist? Musician. If you don't have one that is absolutely fine. Whoever it may be, it is the person you feel personally connected to through thoughts and feelings of 'support' and 'guidance'. If it is several talented artists then great. This is *your experience* so I want you to benefit the most from this adventure. It may be someone you grew up listening to. It may be someone you physically think 'woah!' 'You are a bit of me!' You may have one that you connect with their lyrics on a spiritual level. You don't know 'why' you just '*know*'.

As I am older I look back at my life experiences and the artist I chose for this was always there. His music was very comforting for me at a time I needed those lyrics and words the most. His music related to my experiences. I think and feel as though you can call it a spiritual sort of connection.

I've got my artist. Have you? I can't wait to tell you who mine is. Whoever you have chosen you can do all the practices I speak about but with that talented, inspiring artist in your creative mind. Yep, I am talking about the one we've just talked about but I am also talking about you, my friend. I am going to refer to you as the 'artist' in this chapter. Why? You are starting to paint your magical life and the end result is revealing itself. Shall we do some form of gratitude? I think we both know, that familiar beat to our favourite tunes will sound even better.

Thank you. Thank you ears for being so clear to enable me to listen to this music. When we say 'thank you', when we truly, deeply feel thankful I have a feeling the music will sound even better. Let's thank our freedom of choice. Our freedom to choose the song we want to listen to. Thank you freedom of choice! There are people in this world who may not have such a privilege. So, my little artist, let's bring the lyrics we love to them!

'Don't' by Ed Sheehan is being blasted through my headphones and my feet are starting to twitch. I believe this song has never sounded so good, as it does now. Thanks to the practice of gratitude. If you are listening to a song right now, how does it make you feel? Do you feel good? My body is moving in ways I never realised it could. I am closing my eyes and hearing this beat, feeling it as though I've never heard it before. Although I definitely know the lyrics already, whoops. Girl, feel that song you have chosen. Smile and the artist will emerge.

I went to Stagecoach Performing Arts School for about six years when I was younger. Two of the three parts of Stagecoach were dancing and singing. Two arts I never thought I could do. Honestly. My friends and I laugh still to this day at the moves and notes that we used to create as young girls. I look back and actually this weekly activity contributed to my future. Music. Dancing. Two things I genuinely love now.

In the past I thought I received interesting looks on the dance floor, actually I still continue to dance despite believing this in all those nightclubs. Although, there was a period of time where I did not dance because my confidence disappeared. I am going to be honest though, I can't sing. I mean I can sing but it isn't pretty! I'm going to sing as I write this. Why? It makes me happy. People in the flat next door may think I'm bonkers but I'm going to give it a go. I'll give it a go for you and I.

Okay, I did it. I have replayed 'Don't!' Do you know what feels good? Yeah you got it, artist. Life feels good. The other art was acting at the performing arts school, Stagecoach. My dad used to say I 'belonged on the stage'. Yeah okay, Dad...

Artist, I've just realised something. You know which artist I chose. Uh oh. You are good at getting things out of me, honestly aren't you. I am now starting to tell you stuff without even realising. It reminds me a bit of in 'Mean Girls' when 'word vomit' emerged. If you haven't seen the film it is a term used describing when you say something 'accidentally' and it all comes out at once. No real control over it. You probably knew this anyway didn't you! Such an artist you are. So I've spoken a bit about singing and dancing. As we go through this playlist, I want you and I to focus on that artist we chose. Artist, artists or if you like…Ed Sheeran. Great choices either way.

Artist, do you remember the 'Gratitude' part of this adventure? If you don't or missed that part out, I do recommend going back to the opening pages and taking a moment to read it at some point. I hope you will look back at it and smile with that gorgeous smile of yours. The reason I believe this will hopefully happen is because you will look at the Gratitude section and be able to apply it to your own life. I think and believe you will look at it and know exactly who I am focusing this playlist on. Those few people in your life or in the past. They may be blood relatives or they may not. Either way, they are **your** family. The important word here simply being 'your'. No one else's. They may be related to other people of course, however, this is **your** experience so I want you to focus on you. Even if they are related to other people, or friends of other people. We are talking about your life. Your story. Your adventure. *Our story.*

Let's get started. At the start of this chapter, I asked you to think of an artist or multiple artists that you feel connected to. Have you got them in that magical mind of yours? You know mine is Ed Sheeran. Why you ask? The definite reason, artist, is because I have always connected to him. Not as an artist. As much more. A person. He has very much been a part of my life for six years now. I am so grateful for his support and unknowing friendship. I am going to spend this chapter explaining why.

I hope that from this you believe even more in the magical powers of thinking which ultimately affects how you feel. Apply what I say in this chapter to your own life. No, I can't guarantee you will meet your favourite musician. Especially if they are not present in today's world. Although, I do believe the songs you have been listening to will have a lot more meaning then they ever did before. For you, artist, I have this feeling you are going to be a lot more honest and thus open to how you feel about that incredible artist you chose than I previously was. Lucky artist they are to have been chosen by your wonderful, honest self!

So the talented singer you chose. Who is it? As you know mine is Ed. Who is yours? I think you should write it down so you remember and keep it somewhere. I have a green furry little suitcase box with flowers (don't ask!) of memories that I started when I was in my teens and I have very special things in there. I want you to remember this person. For a long time. How do their lyrics make you feel? There may be a particular song you instantly think of that gives you a certain emotion. I'll tell you mine. 'A Team'. In 2012, I was in hospital. I was admitted into a psychiatric ward. Honestly artist, I was not feeling as good as I am right now. I am not going to go into this because like I said earlier on…I want this book to be positive. I want nothing more than for you to be happy.

Therefore I will paint you a picture instead. I was in hospital for almost six weeks. I did not have Spotify or Itunes then, well if I did I'm pretty sure I didn't want any real proper contact to any form of social media. I was a suspicious patient! My mum kindly gave me her iPod to use. Honestly, I listened to Ed every day. His music was my therapy. He became a friend. I would listen to his lyrics and although I didn't know how or why, his lyrics were very real and comforting.

There was something about the honesty and relatable tone of his lyrics that kept me calm and grounded. I remember hearing the song and I was totally convinced it was about me. It may be totally bonkers artist, but do you know what girl, I am going with it. In the song he says 'They say she's in the class A team. Stuck in her daydream'. He then goes on to sing 'but lately her face seems slowly, sinking, wasting.' I felt this to be very true about myself. I was in an absolute daydream artist but did you know, it is now becoming very obvious as to why I went through what I did. It has made me the honest, strong person I am today.

Thank you 'A Team' and Ed for coming into my life. Through your lyrics I have gained a friend in music. Through your lyrics I have gained a support pal outside of my family. Yes artist, this is my experience but I have a feeling yours could be quite incredible too. Think of that artist you were drawn to. At what point of your life did you start listening to them? That was when your life as a creative artist actually presented itself into real form! Let's continue.

Artist, I have got to tell you something that happened last night. I came across this tape in my flat that I share with my amazing mum. The tape said 'Ellie' on it. I knew it was going to be me speaking. It was me aged about thirteen or fourteen. Singing. Artist. Singing. Goodness me. I haven't heard it since the day I made it. I had created a song. A very 'quirky' song. With interesting phrases and lyrics. I heard it with my mum last night and I promise you this I actually fell to the floor because I was laughing so much. My mum was chuckling away, probably saying in her head I imagine 'What a bizarrely wonderful creature I have created!' In the recording, I then go onto make extremely unique, made up phrases. All at once they come out my mouth. The only comparison I can think of is that video you may have seen online of the gorgeous Jesy Nelson from Little Mix doing that accent. If you have not seen it, do not worry. We will be looking at and exploring the wonderful Jesy soon I'm sure. Hint.

Back to playlist two. On Eddy S. E-Dawg. Ed released the album '+' in 2011. Songs such as 'drunk', 'the city', 'u.n.i', and 'give me love' were very much my daily water. Songs of his became my medication. I would listen to them and little did I know then they were creating my experiences in life. When I got discharged from hospital I felt okay. Okay, not good. I did turn to experiences that did not make me feel better. I drank alcohol and made choices that did not improve my mental health. In Ed's lyrics 'Maybe I'll get drunk again' and yes I would often be in situations where I was 'wishing I was sober.' I thought alcohol would help me, give me confidence. It did not for me at that point in my life. For me personally, it was very much a trigger for not getting better. Alcohol is something people can enjoy but I never saw it as something to 'enjoy' it was more for confidence. I shortly moved to the 'city that never sleeps'. London. The song 'The City' relates more now to that time than I ever knew.

London is a beautiful city. But, I could not keep up at that time in my life when I was not fully well. Physically. Mentally. I did not feel as strong then as I do now to live there. 'London calls me a stranger.' Ed in the last verse says 'This is not my home.' 'And if the city never sleeps then that makes two.' My parents blessed me at this point. Move to London and find your passion. More importantly, get well. I know if I move back to London now I will be able to be less of a 'stranger'.

I had a struggle sleeping there, ultimately ending in me being back in a ward in hospital. Yes, Artist it was only for a few days. This was enough for my parents to realise we had to pack everything up and move. Thank you, Mum and Dad for your incredible awareness of mental health. You know more than you realise. Thank you Ed for being so honest in your lyrics. You are all very special and I don't think or believe you realise how you have actually helped to get me and I'm sure other people to health.

When I was in hospital I met someone who I believe is, still to this day a little special. I remember when I first saw him that day in the canteen. I knew when I first met him he would have an impact on my life. Why, you ask artist? I just knew. I believed it. There was something about the way he carried himself. I wanted to be there for him. Now for the first time in my life I know why.

We connected after hospital in a mental health social group. Honestly, those weekly Wednesday trips to different social venues, especially that snooker hideout spot brought me a lot of support and comfort at the most challenging period of my life. During this time, I really did want this guy to 'give me love.' We would talk for hours over Facebook messenger. I spent a lot of time with him at the YMCA where he was living. Hearing about his experiences which if I'm honest I never really understood. He was in and out of hospital so I will never forget those journeys to Crawley to deliver his favourite 'Tom' bar and give him his cigarettes.

I started listening a lot to Ed when I met this guy in hospital. I felt so much comfort in both these people. Interestingly I look back and physically yes they look very similar, red hair, light skin but it is their honesty and openness that drew me to them. I want you to think about that artist you like. Is it the way they express their experiences through their lyrics or is it that they remind you of someone you know in your life and their lyrics *comfort* you?

When I was at university I got involved with a situation that I can only describe as 'toxic'. I pretty much blamed myself for years because I was totally cringed out about the way I was around one particular guy. I felt shameful that I had not respected who I was brought up to be and done what I thought was degrading myself, chasing that butterfly who wasn't interested in the real Ells, only the drunk one who arrived at the door at the end of a night out. I chased a butterfly, maybe a few and I got nowhere. I couldn't even say this one's name for years without feeling goosebumps, those weird kind of 'don't talk about it' bumps. Even his face made me feel uncertain and nervous. I have memories of being on nights out looking to see if he would be looking at me. He never did.

The only real memory I have of this experience is being at his one night. I had been on a night out and I was drunk calling him asking repeatedly if I could come in. I wanted him to like me. I couldn't understand why I wasn't 'enough'. I was in no real state to have a conversation that night yet be alone with someone. I do remember being called a 'tease' as we were together. Which meant if I was ever called this again my immediate reaction would be to suddenly cease up, in my mind and my body. My spirit too.

Never feel shameful to say the word 'no' if you do not want to do something. It is brave and it is your right. That is why we have freedom of speech my lovely Lioness. The word itself is empowering. You are in charge of your body and what you do with it. The main memory I have of that night is being on the floor of his room. I'm pretty sure I locked myself in the bathroom for the rest of the night. I remember frantically pacing around his ensuite bathroom not knowing where to go. I wanted to hide. Hide from that experience and my mind. I vaguely remember in the morning his housemate saying 'That sounded like an episode of Eastenders last night in your room' to him.

Why? I have no idea. I think there was a lot of shouting. All I know is that it was potentially quite dramatic. I felt scared. Terrified, in fact. I left the next morning or afternoon I'm not sure. Within a few weeks I took a drug because I wanted to escape. I locked myself in the library during the day and tried to study about women in contemporary society. I couldn't work out why the word 'perfect' couldn't be found. It is because it does not exist, Queen. I would then go on nights out which were predominantly drug-orientated to see if I could 'act' in a way he would like. I didn't want to be in this world because I thought it was cringe. I chased that butterfly that did his best to stay clear of me. My dad had to come with me on the train to Leeds to hand in my final draft of my dissertation which was on female identity in contemporary society because my mind had totally run off (the cheeky bugger!) I remember being at my old local train station back home and I was struggling to walk and could hardly speak. I wasn't sure my lovely sunshine mind was ever going to come back. It did!

Was it my fault? No. He was into drugs, I took that drug because I thought it was 'cool'. I thought it might make him 'like me more'. He was into it, so maybe I should do it to impress him. Did it? No. I never blame him for this night. I am grateful I am able to talk about it now. I said to my parents when I came home that something 'bad' had happened at university. It is only now I know what really went on that night. I lost my mind because I was terrified of being with someone that altered how I felt about the lovely world.

This experience led to my self-destructing years. Alcohol. Relationships where I attracted men who did not treat me the way I wanted. All because of my mind and the effects of not having true real self worth or love. Most importantly, I had zero self respect.

I made choices and thus had a few years of experiences that did not bring me the happiness I wanted. The reason being it is a choice I made which happened because of an experience I had. The lyrics of 'Bloodstream' have never felt so relatable, Ed. Artist, my focus on this is because I want to be honest. Yes but I also want you to make choices. Believe in yourself so much that you will attract happy people, events, and situations by choosing the right thoughts. You can make choices.

The reason for telling you about these experiences artist is to show you what we are experiencing in life. I don't believe just happens. It has a reason that it exists. It has been brought into your life for a reason. No matter what, you will learn from every experience. Honestly, I can't emphasise this enough. Do I wish I hadn't been through what I'd been through? Nope. I am so proud, artist. These experiences I have had, brought me into a reality where I am able to confidently share with you. Any experience you are having now will strengthen you. Whether it is positive or not it will make you honestly who you are.

In the loving words of my grandma Oma, experience...TICK! To be honest, my mental health was never helped because in an attempt to protect myself I was never honest with what had gone on in my life which in turn caused less positivity around me. I did fall off the radar at university which people have told me recently and I can respond to this now by saying I was not as happy as I am today. 'Oh you and I ended over u-n-i'. Lyrics that I never related so much until now to my life. Whether it be GCSE pressures, A level, or even university challenges. Artist, I did not finish my degree. I could not sit my last exam and look what that previously less attractive feeling has brought me? I have written a novel. Experiences shape you and make you the magical, empathetic person you are today.

I spent quite a few years listening to Ed, his album 'X' has been there throughout the past couple of years. I now know why. When I hear 'Nina' lyrics I relate to them a lot. 'Part-time lover'. To the guy I knew back at the YMCA where I visited you, I am so grateful for the experiences we had together. I knew I wanted to be there for you but to be honest I needed to help myself first. 'You can make it on your own...' 'Get on a plane'. I certainly did! I connected to a beautiful country, Australia. I wouldn't have been there if it wasn't for that guy I met in hospital.

Yes, we have experiences and moments which we do not like or enjoy. And yet, artist. Being honest with you has made me look at these experiences with real, honest happiness. It has shaped this incredible journey even more.

We went to a wedding a few years ago, maybe five or six years ago. The song 'Thinking Out Loud' was on as my beautiful, old nanny danced with her new husband. My mum said to me in this moment, 'Ells, that will be you one day.'

I genuinely never believed her until now. Thank you, Mum. You are quite something. Thank you to my old Nanny. She is a very special woman and I remember my mum saying she thought this lovely woman had angel wings. This beautiful person was one of the people to visit me in hospital outside of my family. I can't thank her enough for her kindness and support. She is a very special soul.

Artist. I grew up always saying 'Take it back!'. I was notorious to my friends at school for saying these words. If someone said something negative I would say, 'TAKE IT BACK!' The honesty and belief Ed conveys in this song is a little mind blowing. I have just realised Ed and I yes did connect but artist I have a feeling you are present here too. I could write for days about the lyrics of Ed and the real person I met that day in hospital. However, this journey is for you my friend. Yes, you and I - notice I said you first! I am showing an example that if you believe something to be true, any quirky idea, thought, or feeling that it does exist in your life at some point. Ed's song 'Photograph'. It has made me think yes 'loving can hurt'. 'You know it can get hard sometimes'.

I reconnected with the guy I knew from hospital quite recently.

He told me he wanted me to give him a chance. For the first time ever probably with him I had to say no. I said no because I could not be with someone that I cared too much about. He was a friend. He said he felt like 'Stuart Little' where I lived. I know he appreciated my honesty. He drew a picture of me in a castle near where I lived during this time. Honestly, it was incredible. I wish I had kept it but actually not keeping it has helped me heal.

The song 'Photograph'. Beautiful song. Do you agree artist? Let's get a photo girl of that artist you chose. I have mine. Have you got yours? Let's give that musician a huge 'thanks'. I chose one of Ed in a hoody because I once borrowed one off the guy in hospital and 'forgot' to give it back. Haha. He never followed this up. Thank you to him! Although, I think Mum has since got rid of it. Let's look at that photo and smile together. Girl. Thank that artist for coming into your life the moment you needed them most. If they support you and comfort you when you need them then what an artist they are. Thank you to the guy in hospital. I hope that whatever he is currently doing he is happy. I also hope he is continuing with his magical art. Thank you to Ed for being there when I needed a musical artist the most. In his words in "Photograph' 'loving'...'it is the only thing that makes us feel alive'. Ed thank you for guiding me to the 'happier' life we know exists in your most recent album.

To the guy I knew back in hospital. I knew you would impact my life and thank you for being honest and telling me about those cows that were in the park which I definitely did not see but if you believed they were there, I believe you.

Artist. I am emotional. Emotions of happiness. If you believe my experiences which I know you do I hope you can see if you are not okay then that is more than okay. Just tell someone. Honesty got me to where I am. Parents or a support helper can help you. Whoever the lucky person is that you choose. Go with honesty. No feeling, belief, or thought is wrong or too deep for someone you trust. It may not be now or tomorrow. I hope it isn't. I believe if you did have a feeling or uncomfortable thought you would and will do this anyway. You honest artist. The young women of today, you inspire me so much.

Time to naturally close this playlist. I hope you have enjoyed this one. It's getting better and better isn't it my friend...

See ya in the next page/playlist!

T minus...NOT LONG!

E. x

P.S. 'I'll find comfort in my pain...Eraser' - Thank you, Ed Sheeran. You legend. I stopped chasing butterflies. An idea Artist I'm sure we will keep exploring.

Putting Playlist 2 Into Practice

Honesty.

Ultimately, this chapter is all about honesty. I find Ed Sheeran's lyrics very relatable. He talks about experiences such as in 'Bloodstream' taking drugs. I think this is powerful because to touch on a subject like drugs could be a potential risk. However, Ed does it in a way that makes it very relatable to young and older people. He uses his experiences in his life throughout all of his albums and they are honest. He is accountable. He is a very real man. He is down to earth and very genuine; and it is shown through how he communicates through his life, his image, and his wonderful self.

He was homeless but he has shown that with his self-belief and use of his experiences he can relate to the world. That is why Ed Sheeran I believe has done so fantastically. He is real. A normal guy going through normal things that people face in life. He is hugely inspiring because he is so honest. He is not afraid to speak about his life because he knows that people will relate to him. It does really link back to the first chapter because I do believe if you dig a little deeper with Ed's lyrics you can see that he does not always think of himself as being the best guy but he is so humble and through a bit of comedy shines a light on every experience he has had. You may share my feelings about Ed if not that's great too. Who do you look up to? Have you ever looked into their background? If not, I recommend doing this and see what challenges they have overcome.

In relation to my experiences, I know that honesty got me better.

When I saw my therapist September 2018, I was honest for the first time. I told her that I had taken a drug at university and suddenly I felt well. I did not want to be a woman in today's world - I would wear huge jumpers at university. My friend even said to me in first year 'Ellie, we think you have a drinking problem' deep down I knew I didn't. I just wanted to escape which led to me taking that drug.

Ultimately, talking about these experiences honestly has meant I do not feel alone. A problem shared really is a problem halved. If someone else knows what you have experienced they can often look at it objectively - a friend, a family, or even a charity. There is someone always there to hear you and help.

Share with me on Instagram who you look up to and if you relate to any of the challenges they've overcome using #TheSunshineAdventure @eloisaroars

PL3YLIST

'YOU GOT THE POWER'

Hello Jesy, you strong thing.

"With the new day comes new strength and new thoughts."
Eleanor Roosevelt (Summersdale Publishings Ltd).

Girl. GIRL! It's been a page and I promise you this, since we last connected in the previous playlist I have been counting down the seconds until my pen - which by the way has 'sisterhood' on - reaches this page so we can reconnect. I have this sparkly feeling this chapter is going to be an exciting, empowering one. Why you ask? Ever had an experience with a person, maybe a friend or a boyfriend and never been able to make 'sense' of that relationship? It may not have happened yet and if it has we will explore it together through 'Sisterhood'.

Do you remember when you were younger or maybe even now ... where there was/is a band present in your life, it may be any band. Any! For me, it is Little Mix. I wasn't super young but their lyrics and songs have appeared continuously on my Spotify, what I believe to be *unintentionally*. Who have you chosen? It may be a female band, or even a male band that you have spent some time listening to. If it is female yes think of 'Sisterhood' and if a male band apply the exact same as 'Brotherhood'. Either way, this is your magical adventure you are painting so throw on those acrylic paints as you wish. You creative thing. When I was little I adored a range of bands, including the incredible, Spice Girls and Destiny's Child. Or, if you want to use Little Mix in this practice, please do. Be my guest. My special guest. My Sister.

When I mentioned Jesy Nelson in the last playlist, there was a definite reason. I'm going to be calling you 'Sister' in this playlist. I hope that is okay. The reason is you are starting to feel like a sister I never had. I have a brother who is my absolute rock, but I have a feeling there is a sister, sisters, *you* that I never actually knew about... until now.

Sis. I have to be honest. After writing about the video of Jesy doing that accent, I watched it and could not stop smiling. So I have spent the last twenty-four hours mainly bopping my head to the Little Mix classics, thus feeling inspired to tell you. So I did initially structure this chapter, because honestly as we speak, you inspire me more and more. As I type these words on my laptop ready to submit my first draft of the novel, I am speaking with absolute honesty. I did write this chapter with two women in my life in mind, I wrote initially about these lovely ladies. However, things changed for me.

After I completed this magical adventure I reconnected with one of my best friends from back when I was about fourteen. When I started believing in myself and this adventure I knew I wanted these pages to be about honest love for your friends. When I wrote it back a few weeks ago I talked about two good friends of mine who actually I felt like I was doing it for them. I changed this thought. This adventure is for you and I Sister so I have altered these to two women, my best friends when I was in my teens. It feels more real and lovely now as I type this.

If I'm honest it is almost impossible to think of every friend in your life that you see as a 'best friend'. Do you agree? I'm sure you are blessed with a lot of friends. To all my best friends, you know who you are. You are all 'Mixers'. If I were to write about you all, I would be here for years! So. I'm going to focus on three. Although, I think and feel the same to all of my *friends* on a similar 'vibe'.

My aim for this playlist is for you to focus on that lovely band. I will be exploring Little Mix because I believe there was a reason I went to that concert of yours, Little Mix. I cannot wait to tell you why that band you have chosen will become a part of your real life. Let's go sis, 'sister from another mister'. Whoever created this phrase, thank you so much! I find it 'catchy'.

Let's go. 'Le-go!'. I promise you, yes we will look back but only in the most powerful, strong way possible. Why? You may be asking. Sis, you have the absolute *power*. A magical superpower. That is why my friend. In Little Mix's lyrics they sing 'I got the Power!'...' Cause I know just what I'm worth!' Girl, you have maybe not seen or discovered your absolute intrinsic power yet. I believe you know that it is there though.

I can confidently assure you, you do have this 'Power'. You have the 'power' in your life to be whoever you want to be. Of course, there are limitations for people, challenges we face. Actually the only real hold back is not feeling as though you have 'power'. What we doing Sis? You read my mind. Thank your band. Thank you Little Mix you absolutely wonderfully strong bunch of beauts.

So your strong mind is probably asking: why are we doing this exercise? Sister, because not only is it exciting to think of your favourite band as your real life girl 'squad', we are actually going to bring that band into your reality. Eek. There is a reason you chose the band you did. You were attracted to them. They are your 'vibe.' Maybe their songs, their image, their words or even the relationship they have with each other. You may not know how, why but what you do know is that they have been there for a while. No one can argue with that. Although as a sister, I'll be honest I have a feeling you are a bit stronger than you realise. Maybe it's some form of 'Sister Telepathy' I've created, who knows. Let's find out.

Have you got your band? Let's think of them. I wonder who your favourite member is. With Little Mix, for me it is difficult as I find them all equally strong and empowering. Let's make this easier. Has anyone ever said a person in that band reminds them of you? Or maybe you actually look at one particular member and think 'Whey! We are a little similar'. Maybe physically. Maybe emotionally. It could even be Spiritually. On Wikipedia, it says spirituality is 'the quality of being concerned with the human spirit or soul as opposed to material or physical things.' Thank you Wiki! You are ace. Spiritually for me means connecting with someone's soul. This is my personal view on it though. Their energy and aura makes you feel connected. It may be their smile. You connect with them on a level of spirituality. It may be that you look at that person and a word comes into your magical mind such as 'kind' or 'lovely'.

I'll start this off. Little Mix. We have the gorgeous Perrie, we have the stunning Jade, the beautiful Leigh-Anne, and the dazzling Jesy. I am going to have a think. 'Sisterhood' is very much the theme of this playlist. When you think of the word 'Sisterhood' what words and images come to your mind? For me, it is simple. Friendship. I have been blessed in my life with friends. Throughout school and university and into adult life. Every friend I have had in my life has honestly, really impacted me. I imagine it is the same for you. If it isn't, can you count three good friends on your lovely, left hand? If you can, fabulous. If you are feeling this exercise is a bit harder to do then that is more than fine. I want this to be easy for you. I have three sisters that I am going to share with you so you can imagine them being there with you. And do you know what? If you had those friends in mind, I bet they will become even more special Sis, here we go.

I'm going to start with my own version of Leigh-Anne. What a beautiful soul. I do think of a woman, sister in my life when I hear the word 'beautiful soul'. There is no doubt. She is a very special person I have known since I was about eleven years old. We went through three schools together. THREE! Junior school, middle school and then followed each other to Sixth form. I think of her and I think of my left arm. She pretty much holds me up when I can't hold myself up. This woman is so easy to talk about because of her nature. The easiest in my life to be honest. Every time we communicate it is effortless.

I could pretty much say anything to her and I know she would probably laugh. This girl, actually woman now, has always been popular. Everyone loves her. How could you not. Her laugh is contagious. She does a little giggle and you literally cannot help but mirror it back to her. With your 'left arm' friend, how does she make you feel? For me, it is a lot of laughter. A lot of belief also. I don't think she actually realises how great she is. I hope through these words she can start to believe me when I tell her that she infects my life with happiness.

This woman was a brave soul, she visited me in hospital. She visited me in hospital, girl. When I was not feeling as good as I am today. She was there. What a woman. I remember her coming into hospital. I was so happy to see her honestly. She sat opposite me and smiled.

This sister never judged what I was saying. Even if I was telling her peculiar beliefs I had about the world. I would tell her stories about the ward and even when she just looked at me, I knew I was going to be okay. I had her. We went separate ways at university. I still visited her and she did for me too. When I was writing this adventure I went and saw her at her parent's house. The house she has always lived in. With her incredible parents who I see as family. The house is the same. The feelings for them all are still the same.

This woman is one hell of a cool chick. She is so calm and collective. If I am with her, I actually mediate my quirkiness and chill out massively. I try to. From nights out, to pick 'n' mix being our true love in life. To videos being made on webcam, singing along to 'Dear Diary' by Britney Spears, I'll save the best one until last. This gorgeous person knows why. Harry Potter. Yep. I said it. Haz Pots. We genuinely know a scene from Harry Potter. She is the pick to my mix and I can't actually thank her enough for never leaving my life. You are ace and deserve some sort of gold star for being a true, best friend. This angel came with me to get my first tattoo when I came out of hospital. Something I have a feeling we will be speaking about later in this adventure.

Sista. Let's go to the next queen. I'm going to talk about Jade. Choose your second member. If your chosen band has more or less members apply the exact same experience I am expressing to that lovely bunch, to **your experience**. Jade. What do I think of her? She's obviously a kind soul. You can just tell, can't you. It may be that lovely smile that member has. There are words I'm instantly thinking of with Jade. Sweet. She looks so sweet and kind but I have this feeling there is something more to the sweetness. She looks very strong. Behind those sparkly eyes. I think there is actually a bit of a warrior. Whether or not she knows how strong she actually is I don't know, but I see it and very much believe it. Hey to my friend who I see as Jade. My real life Jade. What a lovely 'freckly' girl she is. Now woman.

So I met this little cute thing at secondary school. She was one of my best friends. We went on holidays together. We did a lot together. Wrote letters, cards, danced to High School Musical with another of our best friends. Ate custard creams with our tea. Ate Pringles with

Coca Cola. We visited families together. She was very much a sister to me. We reconnected a couple of days ago after twelve years. Twelve years and we still remember each other's lives. Amazing right? That's why this girl, woman is so easy to talk about. It was always a natural friendship with her. I remember when we were young she said to me 'Simba from the Lion King is so fit!' I laughed with her at this. She was very right.

I told her about this belief she had the other day and she said she was glad she looked beyond looks, more to a personality. Correct, Frecky. You always had a heart of gold. This is very much shown in how successful you are today with what you are doing. I found out she is a Director of a company. Honestly, it doesn't actually surprise me. Someone so kind deserves a lot of success. Go girl. Just try to avoid those mosquitos. Much of our youth we would talk about boys. Two boys in particular. They were pretty much our daily water. This woman actually told me this week that the one I liked was my boyfriend for a bit. I actually don't really remember this. I knew I was very 'puppy love' into him but actually he was my boyfriend! He poured apple juice into his Cheerios in the mornings, instead of milk. Thank you for never judging me Frecks for my quirky ways. You were definitely quirky too. 'Nibbs', 'Eve' were the nicknames you gave me. Dotty B. Thanks for that one. I love it! My grandmother was called Dorothy so yes Dorothy is my middle name. You abbreviated it to make it sound cool, so thank you.

Sis. Let's grab our third member of our girl squad. You ready? I most certainly am. Perrie. What we thinking? Okay. Yes. She's obviously absolutely gorgeous. That sparkling blonde bombshell. Who is your final member? And or members? Hint. We do have one more coming up though. Your own Perrie. She oozes a little bit of greatness I believe. Am I right? She is that friend in your life who has been there from day one. Okay. Is it just me or is there something a bit 'angelic' about our Perrie? Yes, it could be the blonde hair but I have a feeling there is a little more to this, sister.

The Perrie in my life is a genuine angel sent from somewhere. I am totally convinced that this girl has wings under her little petite arms. Surely. Think of that friend in your life that yes, is your right arm. Who honestly makes you feel a bit 'out of place' when she is not there. My Perrie is currently in Australia for a bit, but Sis, let's bring her to this experience. Where is yours right now? If they are near you, then lucky you!! (And them of course). If not we can bring them here and thank them.

It may sound 'quirky' but actually thanking them for their continuous support and love could make you feel as though they are actually here. It may be a photo. It may be a memory you think of. Go there. No delay. Mine is at sixth form. To be honest when I think of school I think of this angel. Along with our 'Timone' but I have a feeling Timone may be mentioned later in the book. Just a feeling. Whether it was singing to Amy Winehouse or dancing to Beyoncé, or lapping on 'pearl and shine' Nivea lip balm you have never brought me a dull moment. We will be friends together, forever. I will be there rocking with you in that chair in the homes when we get old, I promise you that.

Like we always said, we were born in the wards next to each other (yeah right!). No matter where in the world our adventures take us next you are one loyal 'toad'. Thank you Perrie for being a woman representative of the gem I get to call my 'bestie'. 'She my bestie, bestie, bestie'. Thank you Yungen! A great song. To the angel, you wrote on a postcard once that said 'When life gives you lemons' on the back you said 'we will squeeze them and make lemonade together!'

Okay sis, we have our last member of 'Little Mix' to bring to the table. As you look or listen to that band you chose, was there a member you instantly thought 'hmmm...people have said that I remind them of this person?' Mine is the dazzling, strong Jesy. I remember when I was with my ex-boyfriend I said 'babe, out of all the Little Mix group, who am I most like?' I would spend days just lying on his sofa watching music videos. There was little else to do when he was fixated on his gaming screen haha. He replied saying 'That one' pointing at Jesy, to be fair to him he did not know their names I don't think.

Little did I know then, I was asking him a fundamental question that would add that extra sprinkle of fairy dust over this adventure, something I never dreamed I could create. So the member, 'gal' you chose as yourself to complete that empowering dream team, who is it? I'd love to know every single positive word, image, even feeling you have towards them. I bet you are going to create an artistic masterpiece Sis, how do I know? I believe in you. I believe Little Mix do too.

Jesy. Visually, I am going with she is obviously beautiful. That's a given. She has striking eyes that compliment her lovely face. The more I can see Jesy, the more beauty I am seeing. I believe she has an incredible figure. She wears clothes I believe that always make a statement in a truly great and empowering way. She is a woman and is not afraid to show how inspiring she is. Now that you have got your members visual description done. Let's have a think about their personality and their 'aura'. The personality that makes them who they really are. For Jesy, I am saying fun. I believe she looks like a lot of fun. Someone you would want to be around. Not just for her smile but there is some kind of warm, aura around her that I believe makes me want to give her a massive 'Sunshine' hug! Sis, do you realise what this exercise is doing? The person you chose had to bring positivity to you. I wanted it so much so you could liken yourself to that talented artist. Your beautiful self. Your true self.

If I am linked to someone in 'Little Mix', I am honoured. More importantly, thank you Jesy for being not only beautiful on the outside but very much on the inside too. Sis. Your turn. All the positives you saw in that artist, whether it be their honesty, their loyalty, their beauty or their compassion, thank them and please thank yourself. There was a reason you were attracted to that specific person. I hope you are smiling. I am. Let's smile together.

Before we end this chapter Sis, I promised you we would talk about a relationship you may not have been able to make sense of. I hope it has been fun so far but let's turn it up a 'notch'. Let me reveal why. Have you ever had a relationship, boyfriend perhaps or even a girlfriend that you have always held less 'positive' feelings for? It may not have happened yet in your life but if it has please enjoy this moment. This is to do with a romantic relationship you have had or may have in the future that you can look back at and apply this same experience to.

Enjoy this moment. I will. If it hasn't happened yet, please enjoy this too. Either way, this is supposed to be a fun exercise to do. Before we start it I have to refer to Little Mix's recent songs 'Woman's World' what a beautiful song. 'And if you can't see that it's gotta change, only want the body and not the brains.' For so many years I would go to the gym. Years Sis. Aged twenty-one upwards after I fell ill. The sole thought in my head was I thought it would make men like me and my body. Physical exercise is something I genuinely love. I now do it for me. To make myself love me, that little bit more. A sprinkle of magical 'self-love'. It's a good 'medicine' to take. I used to train at the gym because I thought that 'perfect' body would bring me the man of my dreams and happiness. Actually no, do you know what brought me a good feeling? Writing. Using my brain. Which I believe you do too. You're reading a book. A sign of definite intelligence and creativity. Connecting with you has given me a lot of 'good vibes, good life' (Vex King - 'good vibes, good life book). Thank you Vex King.

This is coming from a girl who had about fifteen years of self-doubt. It is only now that I am realising everything I have been through has actually made me the strong person I am today. This is so true for you too honestly. Any less positive feeling you have about yourself you can change. You just have to think of your positives. There will be a lot for you I believe. One positive thought or feeling about yourself can lead to more. More! It may be that time your friend said 'Wow! You are so kind for giving me that birthday card.' Big or small girl, you have lovely qualities I'm sure that other people would love to have. Give yourself a little 'thanks'. *Own it.*

So it is the end of this playlist, sis. We have arrived. I have saved the best until last. When you think of that band what is the first song that comes to mind and you literally jump off your chair because you feel so empowered? When I broke up with my ex-boyfriend, it was not fun. Guess what? We are not going to talk about that relationship right now. Why? Same reason as throughout the adventure. This is solely a happy adventure. We ended the relationship a few years ago and I had to go to his gorgeous parent's house. I needed to pick up a ticket he had kindly bought for me and two friends. A ticket for myself and two friends to go see 'Little Mix' at Twickenham Stoop.

Sis, before I reveal the song and before you play yours. Get comfortable. Get your dancing shoes on and grab your microphone. Let's give a little 'gracias'. I feel this will be quite a moment! For me, thank you to every single friend I have made in my life. There is not one that has not impacted my life in some way. Thank you to the gorgeous two sisters that came with me to this concert, you were so supportive and when I hear this song I remember us screaming and dancing to this song in particular. I genuinely have shivers as I type this. Thank you to 'Little Mix' for being such strong, powerful women of today's world. Last but not least thank you to my ex boyfriend for these tickets to an incredible show. Sis, you ready? Let's sing together the loudest, we have ever sung to...Yes. You got it in one. 'Shout out to my ex!' Over to you, girl.

P.S. 'You made my heart break, and that made me who I am.' Although I have a feeling that these kind of experiences form a type of 'Black Magic'.

E. x

Putting Playlist 3 Into Practice

Strength and power.

This chapter is quite simple really - the power of friends and having a team. Talking, supporting, empowering, uplifting, encouraging and being grateful for the women you have in your friends that you call your 'girl squad' - or 'boy squad' - Little Mix - 'Woman's world' also sums up why I think they are great for our young women. Empowering other women empowers yourself and encourages other females to speak up and be brave about who they are.

However you identify and whomever your friends may be, make sure they are for you and supportive. I have had many friends throughout my life and I do genuinely feel blessed for everyone that has had an effect on me. Although an effect is there for a reason. Good or bad. For you, I would suggest you write a little note, maybe even a list of the main friends in your life who have impacted you the most. For me, personally I have found that counting my best friends on one hand has meant so much more than having multiple friends who I'm not sure I could just call and say, 'I need your advice right now' or simply, 'are you free to talk?'

With this list of your top friends; be it boys or girls you could write down positive things about every single one of them. I know I discuss women a lot in this novel but actually it is the men in my life too who I go to if I want advice or support. Including members of my family.

Positive ideas about friends will bring them even closer to you. For example, you could write simply that they helped you by sending a song, or that they visited you at a time you really needed them, or they look at you when you are feeling terrible and tell you that you still look beautiful. A friend who you may not see for years but the minute you see them you know they never really went away. This is a positive exercise and I believe if you do have some feelings towards people which make you feel less good about *yourself* then write that too. A time of reflection is important when it comes to self love. If you focus on the good, more of the good will come back to you. Your true, honest friends are, in fact, a mirror of yourself.

Strength and power comes from within, of course, by reaching out to the right kind of people in times of need. I have learnt that I am a better friend when I am strong in myself and focusing on the people who I believe will always be there for me when times get tough. Friendship at the end of the day is actually a reflection of how you feel about yourself.

Love yourself first, be your friend first and then you are able to love your girl/boy squad and be there for them when they need or want you to be. #TheSunshineAdventure @eloisaroars

PL⁴YLIST

'THANK YOU, NEXT'

Girl, girl. GIRL! How are we feeling? Hello Ari, you beautiful thing.

'To love oneself is the beginning of a life-long romance.' - Oscar Wilde (Summersdale Publishers Ltd).

I have yes, followed Ariana Grande's music for a while. It may be the same for you. It may not be! Either way, great. I hope you don't mind if I talk about her in this one - there is a definite reason why I want to.

Not sure about you but after the last playlist I am feeling a little empowered! I have a feeling that last song made you feel good? Even if you hadn't gone through a break up, I hope this book stays in your life and you can apply that last classic to any relationship. Even if it is aimed at a friend and non-romantic relationships.

Okay. Playlist four. It's getting juicy and sweet now, don't you think?! As I have said before I am experiencing this magical adventure with you. So it would be natural for me to explain what I am currently going through. To show you that if you feel and believe in something, then you are likely to be right. Trust that lovely little gut of yours. People often would say this to me and I never really understood what they meant. However, girl I have a feeling we are going to explore this a little more in the next couple of playlists.

Right. I have a question for you, girl. Before I ask this question, I am going to explain how this playlist came about. To be honest, the first time I heard about Ariana was through my best friend who I mentioned before. My 'Perrie' remember? The angel. Yes, that girl. I miss her face every day but I am seeing her soon. Woohoo! We were at school together for a large part of our lives. At sixth form we met this absolute 'worldie'. This woman's nickname is Timone, she has been gifted the name Timone because she reminded us of the character from the 'Lion King', as she is full of a lovely positive energy.

About a week or two ago, maybe even before I randomly played my beautiful mum 'Thank u, next' by the stunning Ariana. Yes. The one and only. Grande. I listened to the lyrics for the first time properly with my mum. I promise you this, girl I saw hope. I saw self-belief and my gosh I saw a serious amount of inspiration. I said to my mum, 'what a message!' Ariana symbolises for me absolute self-belief and self-love. Natural, effortless beauty. Obviously, I knew then there was a reason I was drawn to this beaut. Not just for her external 'goddess' like image but for her internal radiance she brought to my life through her music and words.

To my ex-boyfriend, I knew that day when you paused your gaming station which you never did, to watch this incredible soul and woman that was appearing on your television screen. I had a feeling she would affect the world very positively. If she could make you stop gaming, she could do anything! Haha. An initial 'ugh' moment of what I thought was me being suspicious of my boyfriend drooling over Ariana, actually it was the moment I would remember this woman would be an absolute inspiration to young women all across the world.

In this relationship I look back and I know that if I had listened to my lovely gut I would have avoided the heartbreak of this experience. On my birthday, I discovered that another woman had been involved in the relationship. 'Ells, let us take a selfie' on my birthday night out....as the phone was pulled up I saw a message. I asked who it was and I got told it was a man. The picture did not show this. His response was that it was men dressed up in drag. Thank you to the beautiful Ariana Grande's music because it has shone a light on experiences with men, her music makes me feel enough and why I value honesty and gratitude so much in relationships. Listen to that beautiful gut of yours Girl, it will never lie to you. We are enough.

I'm going to be calling you Ari, in this chapter. I hope that's okay. The reason being I believe you, yep you have a lot to feel inspired about girl. I mentioned Timone earlier, I saw her today. We connected for the first time probably properly since school. I lost my way a bit when I went to university as you know girl. However, this little delight has been there throughout. We just hadn't been able to connect until now because my mind had ran away. I have had amazing friends that have been there for me. Although, with this one there is something about the way she carries herself with me. When I saw her today, I just knew there was a reason we were supposed to reconnect. Both of our eyes filled with tears. She had come to see me when I had just come out of hospital in London and if you know there is a genuine friend who has a smile that gets bigger when you smile or their face scrunches up when you are sad. Choose them for this playlist.

Who's yours, Ari? It may be that friend or even a relative. Maybe a neighbour with whom you look at and you idolise a little. Okay. Yes. Timone is absolutely gorgeous on the outside but she is stunning on the inside also.

I had to tell her about the adventure today. It felt natural. Timone is one of the few people to know about this adventure. It was effortless to say the words to her. I knew I wanted her to know. The thing that prompted me was that she said 'Ells, I can see you talking about your experiences with people.' Okay. So we have two women. 'Perrie' and 'Timone'. Girl, Ari, who are yours? The reason I am asking is because I believe whoever you chose, there is a definite reason. Whatever it is that they symbolise obviously inspires you. Timone replied to my announcement to her at brunch saying 'Ells I will be at the front of the book signing line.' I never felt this until now, but I have this little sparkly feeling that artist you chose, for me Ariana who is similar to the person in your life you look at, actually in fact looks at you in a very similar way to how you see them. Just this feeling, a 'vibe' I get.

Thank you so much Timone for that day. You bought lunch and I deliberately did not thank you, I wanted to thank you here. You have no idea how much you have inspired this playlist. Back to you, the reader. Ari. Are we ready to sprinkle a little bit of a 'dangerous woman' on to this adventure with us? So we can bring Ariana to this playlist. Same. I thought you might say yes. This is going to be one hell of a chapter girl, Ari. I am literally sitting at the edge of my seat. Ready for some 'sweetener' to be added to that cup of delicious tea? Me too, let's go, girl.

Ari. Before we get started I have to tell you about the morning I have had. I'll give you some background information. FBI style. Yesterday, I got a phone call from a friend in the morning and honestly it really worried me. I called her back and we spoke but she was not feeling good. I then received some messages that worried me even more. I felt panic run through my body. I did message her sister to make sure she was with someone. I was visiting my parents so I told them I would be off WhatsApp but to call me on my mobile if they needed me.

If I'm honest girl, I felt pretty unsettled from this experience. This is a very honest experience. It is how I felt that day I saw her post on Instagram 'positive vibes' but when I asked her she said she was 'average'. We spoke the next day on the phone, where she said 'you were not there for me' I honestly burst into tears. All I could think about that Sunday was her. Girl. Ari. In the past, I have had a few situations with friends very similar to this. I have tried everything in my power to make that person feel better. However, what I have learnt is that the only person that is truly going to make that person better is them. It's a hard reality to face up to because I have always taken on other people's emotions. I've always been quite sensitive if I'm honest but I have realised it actually means sometimes I care too much about other people and take on their experiences. So after the phone call I knew, just knew what would make me feel better, what would make me smile. Of course, it is writing to you but I didn't want to write about my 'woes' I wanted to write what helped me.

I had a certain feeling that a few things were about to happen to make me smile a lot. I also, before I go on, found a quote this morning. I have no idea how, when, or why this quote appeared in my search engine on Google but I promise you it did. 'Don't chase people. Be yourself, do your own thing, and work hard. The right people, the ones who really belong in your life, will come to you. And stay.' Thank you to the great Will Smith for bringing these words into my life. You hero. For me, I have realised no matter how much I try to make someone happy I have learnt today that you are able to be strong and happy for others when first you are strong and happy in your own skin. Girl. Ari. Remember that 'gut' I was talking about earlier. If something does not feel right or comfortable, listen to your gut and I assure you that negative thought or feeling will evaporate when you start to listen to what your body and mind is saying to you. Just thinking of something that makes you smile, it will make you feel better. It is as simple as that.

Ari. So we mentioned the two special ladies I have in my life at the beginning of this playlist. After speaking with Timone I knew she would inspire this playlist. The other angel inspires me on a regular but I physically was with Timone. The angel was definitely with us in spirit. When Timone radiated with happiness when she saw how happy writing to you made me, it made me realise the beauty of this friend of mine is mirrored in what she believes to see in me. Thank you to Ariana for representing what every young woman is capable of. Natural beauty. Ari, you. Let's start looking at that beauty that is not just outside of you but inside too which exists when you believe. Your inner beautiful soul.

I said at the start of this my angel of a best friend introduced me to the lyrics of Ariana Grande's music. She actually posted a picture back when I was with my ex-boyfriend saying 'hiya EDBD, hiya Ariana'. If this is not someone saying we think you are amazing, then I don't know what is girl, Ari. The artist you chose for this chapter. Who is it? How does their music make you feel? Think of a few songs of theirs, listen if you can and really feel what they are saying. As I said, I am bringing Ariana here because I knew she was an inspiration. I didn't realise how much until now. I have a little feeling we are going to find out in this playlist why. Whoever you chose, think about what they symbolise. How their music makes you feel and I believe a feeling of magic will begin to happen for you. In Ari's words, 'don't you worry about a thing, we're gonna be alright!' Yes to my two 'toads'. Yep, we called ourselves the three toads at school. I was number two. Timone number three and the angel number one. We always competed for number one but actually I think we all know we are joint number ones in our own way, toads. To these two women I know you will understand this, grab your pearl and shine and let's bring a bit of 'pma' to this playlist. Positive Mental Attitude. We used to say this a lot in sixth form.

I am going to be looking at Ariana's first album that I was attracted to. I do have to admit I love all her albums. Truth. And, for some reason 'Sweetener' is calling my name! *Our* names. Take a look at your artist's first album. I wonder which one you are drawn to first? Through this playlist, I am going to be talking about relationships with men and how their individual experiences have made me that little bit stronger, with an extra 'bite' of courage. Which will be developing into a 'roar'. Remember earlier I said I knew what would change my mood? I have a little feeling you may find out in a bit why. The reason for talking about all of this is because I honestly feel and believe that I started listening to Ariana more and more because she was relating to my experiences. I bet she can relate to yours as well throughout your life. I am twenty-seven years old now so for you (as my younger sister!) I can see that who you are musically tuned into does, in fact, become a part of your life and experience. There is a magical reason we are listening to that beautiful artist. Ready little sister, Ari? You were born ready!

Here we go. The first song. Every time. Guy number One. So I knew this guy when I was younger. He was at my fourteenth birthday party. When I had my first kiss, with a marshmallow with my first boyfriend. Don't ask girl, I'm not sure why that happened. This guy went out with one of my best friends when we were young. When I matched with him on Tinder I messaged my friend and asked if she thought it would be weird if I met up with him. She laughed. 'No, Ells.' I think she actually found the whole thing quite funny that we had reconnected. I was seeing this guy for a while. The only way I can describe it is, honestly a bit strange. Not him or me but the communication we were having together. When I look back it was much more of a friendship than anything romantic for us both. I think he will agree with me on this. I remember playing this song on repeat during this period. I now know exactly why. 'I get tired of your no-shows. You get tired of my control.'

I remember so many weekends, mainly a Saturday night waiting for him to 'get back to me'. Waiting for him to turn up. 'Waiting' is the only word I think of when I think of this time. He would either turn up late or say he had some kind of 'emergency' such as an appointment with a nurse because he thought his toe might be broken. He drove to me the next day. Whether or not this story was true, it doesn't matter. As I write this, I am actually laughing. So thank you to this guy for your often 'quirky' statements that would come out of your mouth, if I'm honest they never really made much sense to me. At the beginning, we did have a lot of fun together. He was really good fun to hang out with and I felt comfortable with him at the beginning.

'Call on the regular, I get weak and fall like a teenager'. That was literally me. I remember being at one of my friend's houses before a night out. He called me before I went to this night out in London. I was so excitable when he called me, I think he said something along the words of 'Miss Davis, when am I next seeing you?' The way he would say 'Miss' made me feel like a school girl. It reminded me of being young. And yet, during this period of time I noticed I did not feel my best. I remember trying different looks before I would next see him. I always wanted to try and impress him. 'Just when I get on a new wave boy, you look at me'...'I get drunk, pretend that I'm over it, self-destruct' 'act like an idiot'.

I would ask my friends; constantly analysing his messages asking for their advice. Asking for reassurance got me nowhere. I wasn't being true to myself. I would always blame him and take it out on him for making me feel less good about myself. Actually, it was never him that was hurting me, it was me. I wasn't being true to myself. Thank you to this guy for teaching me **'patience'**. More importantly, I am going to thank myself. I'm not sure our relationship was overly genuine for either of us. I always went back to this one. I tried dating other guys but it would end up with me messaging him....'Every time'. He was comfortable at that period of my life. However, as my confidence was still pretty low during this period I knew and believed I wanted something a little more than comfortable. I knew he did too. He introduced me to 'Poke house' a really good food place near me. I did thank him recently for this. I meant that message. The food is epic. I just hope he can take someone there now that he *genuinely* sparkles with.

Okay. GIRL! So I hope you are enjoying this playlist. It is very much about my relationships with men but I just want to show you that if you believe in something it pretty much exists and stares you in the face. It's a lovely little feeling and helps me understand why these relationships did not work out. Let's move on to the second guy. This was someone I only met a few times when I was living in London. I knew I wanted to write about this experience because if I'm honest I could never really make sense of it. It is only now as I write this I completely get it. Although I only saw him a handful of times this one really affected me. It was probably because it was at a critical point of my life. A point I was not feeling as good as I do now. It all makes a bit more sense now as to why we weren't right for each other. We had our first date at Winter Wonderland. It was actually a really fun night. I think it was one of the first times he had been to London. He lived in Nottingham and was a tree surgeon so he was doing some work near me. We also met on an app. I remember him actually asking me that night if I had bipolar. Nope, I did not have bipolar but actually you were right I was not fully well. For a few years I would message him, block him...unblock him. He said to me that London was too far for him to travel to. We both knew deep down we did not have that 'electricity' with each other anyway but I was unwell so couldn't really understand why we were not in a relationship. I was detached from real life. When I listen to 'break up with your girlfriend, I'm bored' I think of this guy.

He told me he had a girlfriend when we were messaging each other a few years later. I was at a point in my life where I was not satisfied with my mental state. Not feeling so positive. I used to think very similar to what Ariana says in this song. 'I know I shouldn't think about it.' 'Then I realise she is right there.' 'And I'm at home like "damn, this ain't fair".

I do have to admit I don't think we should have been messaging each other but actually we were never going to see each other again and we both knew that deep down. Thank you so much to this guy for not breaking up with your girlfriend. I knew that was never a thought of yours. You have obviously found honest true love. We were never on the same 'vibe' were we! When I think of the few times we spent together, I do actually see 'pain'. I was back in hospital during the period of seeing him. Okay, it was only for about five days but that was enough. I knew I was not in the right mental state for a relationship with anyone. I knew I wanted to wait until the right person would come along to restore my faith in what I believed love to be when I was young. A pain-less, happier 'sprinkle' of honest love.

Girl. Ari. 'Imagine'. Remember in this chapter my mood quickly changed today? I did something that I deep down knew and believed would undoubtedly bring me a smile. As I type this up on my laptop a sudden 'wave' of relaxation came over me. An effortless smile. The final guy. So, I met this guy in November 2018. I am going to keep this one short but very, very sweet. I have a little feeling, a 'vibe' he may be mentioned again in this adventure. It is February 2019 as I write these words. I've known this one for four months now. 'Took a deep breath like ooh!' I used to say to my friends at school and I think to people at university that my 'dream guy' would be a blonde, rugby type physique boy. Personality I wasn't sure of in my younger years. I never thought I had a 'type' as such. I used to brush that question off when people would ask me. Then this guy came along. Physically, he was what I wanted. Being with him taught me that I was able to feel a type of **'love'**. Or maybe it was just 'hope'. I knew deep down I wanted to 'dig deeper' beyond the looks or the visually what I perceived as 'perfect' man. I'm sure we can explore this later.

So Ari, you. I hope you have enjoyed this chapter. It is coming to a gentle close now. I have shared these three experiences with you because I wanted to show you that through patience, pain and love something better happens. Self-love. I do not want to use any negative words in this adventure but actually the word 'pain' is a feeling that can be cured through altering your mind set or thought. Changing a certain song. In Ariana Grande's songs, 'Thank you, next' and '7 rings' she conveys a beautiful once girl, now woman. She thanks her ex's. What a woman. I thank all my ex's. There is one in particular I have not actually brought to the table. The one I was in a long-term relationship with. I did mention him in the previous chapter. Even so, I actually thank this ex the most. Thank you so much to him for ending the relationship. It was the love I dreamed about. Ariana more importantly thanks herself. Girl. Let's give ourselves thanks. A huge massive, self-loving thanks. Even if you have just been reading these words and not able to apply to your life right at this moment in time, you have created this experience with me, I want you to see that you can actually look at previous negative relationships and see a lot of positivity. You made this happen, girl.

Ariana is so gracious in 'Thank u, next' I don't know what you're thinking but I believe Ariana is a person that has been through one hell of a lot in the past couple of years. I feel that is a bit of an understatement. Despite the pain she has experienced, she is an expression of a beautiful soul. A soul of inspiration. Through her voice, her lyrics, and her image she is a lovely person. I think you know what lyric I am referring to here, if not here it is. 'I've learned from the pain...turned out amazing'. Yes, Ariana Grande you most certainly have. For this reason, this playlist had to be on you, you beautiful thing. Your music is hugely influential. It makes sense to my life and I'm sure it does for a lot of young women in today's world.

In Ariana's song '7 rings' she sings 'been through some bad sh*t, I should be a sad b*tch'... 'my smile is beaming', my skin is gleaming'. Girl, Ari, the reader, women, girls, you. Let's thank Ariana Grande for symbolising not only beauty but absolute grace and compassion. If Ariana Grande can do it, girl, we can! Let's conquer the world. I'll see ya in the next playlist. Buzzing to connect again with you would be an understatement.

E.x

P.S. Remember... 'thank u, next'.

Putting Playlist 4 Into Practice

Self love.

Experiences and relationships with men for me have shaped how I view myself. For years, I had very low confidence and self esteem - I did not like my body, my face or anything about myself. I used to critique myself in the mirror - genuinely using words like 'you are fat' 'you are ugly' 'you are not worthy', this was my dialogue for a very long time. When I started writing the book I did develop self love which honestly has changed my life. It has flipped my brain into positive thinking. I look in the mirror now and I say 'I am beautiful', 'I am enough', 'I approve of myself' (Louise Hay/Marisa Peer).

It was not a surprise, I was involved in relationships that did not make me feel good. What you think really does attract how you feel and the experiences you have (Buddah teaches this a lot - 'All that we are is the result of what we have thought' - Gautama Buddha taken from Google). It is only now that I have self love, care, and appreciation that I am attracting the positive people into my life. It is better to have less people but the right people. People who truly make you feel good.

Ultimately, this chapter is focusing on the soul the most. Ariana Grande has obviously had her serious dark moments - she is such an inspiration to women I believe. No matter your past - if you have self-belief and love then you can conquer. Your past does not need to define who you are today and going forward.

Self love = self care so today I want you to write a message to yourself in your mirror. Mine says, "I am enough."

Share a photo of what yours says over on Insta with the #TheSunshineAdventure and tag me @eloisaroars

PL⏵YLIST

'SIGNED, SEALED, DELIVERED'

Hello Stevie, you independent thing.

'Only in the darkness, can you see the stars.' - Martin Luther King (Summersdale Publishers Ltd).

GIRL! What is going on. I loved sharing the last chapter with you. It was a lovely playlist...am I right? I hope you agree. If not, this could be awkward! Hopefully more of a 'quirky' vibe. I have woken up today and what a DAY! What a life. The magic in our lives I believe is starting, well not starting, it is flowing. Through the magical currency of that lovely river. Ready for the next playlist? The structure of this playlist was easy. No, it was effortless. For this playlist, I would like to focus on one artist. I know in previous chapters I have said think of an artist you chose but as this adventure develops we are becoming quite a pair. You and I. If you want to think of a separate artist from this one, who let's be honest, is an absolute legend then please do. So, in this chapter I will predominantly be focusing on the great, the wonderful person that is..... Hold up! You will find this out shortly. When I bring you this artist to the table you may actually choose them. Just a little feeling I have.

So this playlist is going to be focusing on that legendary bunch you call your family. Do you remember in the playlist about honesty, with Ed Sheeran...I said my aim was to start thinking about our

thoughts as a playlist. I read this to one of my best friends the other day. My mum. Yes, she believes in the magical adventure a lot but I came to a realisation this morning. I jumped out of bed. I had breakfast with her. I started thinking, probably singing in my head. When we talked about this book I was sharing everything with her. Oversharing. Something I have done for twenty-seven years to be honest. Relationships. Boys. Actually health too. Today, this changes.

Yes, my mum has been incredibly supportive of this adventure. However, I realised today, the best gift I can ever give to my family is independence. Mum, is my role model. Our love is forever. For now, I need to keep the adventure between you girl and I. Sharing with other people at this point about the content will maybe hold me back a bit. The best writing I get done is when I am independent with you so I can actively focus on this dance on my own. We do need to give a big thank you to my mum for this playlist. This woman introduced me to the 'King' of what I believe is of music who gives me a 'happy bug'. Girl. Drumroll, please. Yes, I am doing an 'air drum' back to you as I speak. Stevie Wonder.

Girl. I am going to call you Stevie in this chapter. I hope that's okay. The reason being that you may or may not know who Stevie is. I hope you don't mind. If you do not who Stevie is, that is more than fine. I will 100% bring his words to these magical pages. The reason I find Stevie so inspiring is because his music is sensational. He is also blind. Blind but has created unstoppable music. He is in my opinion a musical genius. I think when I share with you the songs that have impacted my life you will very much agree with me. I think you are also sensing this is going to be quite an inspirational playlist. You are correct girl, Stevie.

Put it this way, I am yet to see a photo of Stevie where he is not beaming with a smile. I have absolutely fallen head over heels with not only Stevie as a musician, but as a person. Girl, he embodies happiness. He has created songs that give my life a lot of meaning. It is impossible to only choose a few songs to make us both smile in this playlist. And so I am going to pick out the ones that have the most meaning for me and I hope for you too. Although, for you Stevie, of course you can independently look if you are able to at his albums and songs. There are so many and I just know there will be certain ones that make your face feel that little twitch, making that dazzling smile appear even bigger. Before we start, let's give thanks to the inspirational person that Stevie Wonder is. Ready to bring him to the chapter girl? Same! Mr Wonder. Hello you.

So the first song I have been magnetically attracted to is 'Sir Duke'. Girl, Stevie, the first lyrics are 'music is a world within itself, with a language we all understand'. Little did I know when my mum first introduced me to Stevie Wonder's music she was actually shaping my experiences and support system. I have always loved music yes, but I never thought it would shape my life so much. Are we ready for a bit of realism, girl…Stevie?

I had my first panic attack when I was at secondary school. I was sixteen years old. I was in Physics. Never really liked science, if I'm honest. And yet, it was not science that made me feel 'weird'. No. The loss of the kindest, loveliest, gentle giant in my life. My Opa. Which is Dutch for Grandad. He was Dutch. I never knew what had caused my panic attack really until recently when mum and I were talking about that day in Physics when she picked me up in my green and red tartan kilt and we went to McDonalds to get a brown plastic bag to help regulate my breathing.

We lost Opa yes. However, on the 27th January 2019 I was able to reconnect with him at the Harry Edwards Healing Sanctuary. I had no idea I was a spiritual person. I never really 'understood' Spirituality. I thought it was about connecting with things that were not there when I was young but actually this experience became very evident this day that I was very spiritual. My mum always thought I was but this day it became very evident to me in my existence. Guess what else happened this day? Yes Stevie, I started writing to you. Fate? Coincidence? Spiritual? Quirky? Whichever word you believe to be true, then it is right for you. I believe you. For me it is actually, 'Magic'. I never believed in the magic of life to be honest. I had thirteen years of anxiety. How could I possibly believe in this world being 'magical'. It is only now that I am writing this that actually it all kind of makes sense now. I lost you Opa yes but you have actually always been here, watching and guiding me to health and happiness. I have had a lot of factors that have contributed to me getting better. My therapist being a big part of that. That day I reconnected with Opa, I started writing this adventure that evening.

Opa would tell us as kids that he was apart of the *'magic circle'*, he spent most of his days telling jokes or bringing humour to the dinner table. Opa would hug us all. He was and is the warmest gentle giant I have ever known. Opa, there is something about your smile that will always make me smile. It reminds me of Stevie Wonder. I love you and there's no doubt to me that you are there bringing those jokes and warmth to this playlist. Thank you Opa, for believing in magic and telling us as kids that it was real. I never really believed you until I started writing to the young women of today's 'Wonderful World'.

Whilst we are on this subject of Opa. I see similarities between him and Stevie. Also you and I. The smile. The humanity. The love and belief. No, I have not physically met you but I know for a fact you have a wicked smile. I bet it is ace. It is just this little feeling I have. A smile honestly for me makes someone beautiful. So keep it up friend!

So girl, Stevie before we carry on, a few years ago I lost eighty percent vision in my left eye. Yeah. It flipped my world upside down, it went a bit 'wonky.' Thank you to the man, we will call him J for spotting my sight loss that day at the optician. You told me not to panic but as I was rapidly losing my vision I needed to swiftly get on my way to St George's hospital. Stevie. All you need to know about this is yes medication did help. Honestly, what truly helped this recovery was improvements with my physical health. For me personally, I was not happy at the weight I was. I knew deep down my body could not cope with the rapid weight gain going from around nine stone to sixteen in a matter of a couple of months.

Thank you to my eye for repairing. Thank you health for returning. Thank you to the NHS. Thank you Stevie Wonder for actually being there since I was young. You have shown me how inspirational you are as a person. You are human. You do not have your own sight and you look happy every time I see a picture or hear a song of yours. You have sprinkled your loveliness over the world and my aim for this playlist is for us to sing and dance in honour of your greatness. You have done this all yourself and for that you are an independent, inspiration Mr Wonder. So are you Stevie (Lioness).

So at the start of this playlist I did say let's think about family. For you, it may be blood relatives. It may be your friends, they ultimately can be the family you choose for this. Whoever your collection are, think of this clan and I can guarantee you will experience even more love and appreciation for these special people, especially when you give them a little 'thanks'. When I look back at the years if I'm honest I don't think I said those two words, 'thank you' enough to people. It is something I do now everyday. Whether or not these people know this I don't know but in my mind I thank everyone that is affecting my life at whichever moment of the day it is. It may even be someone walking past on the street that is clearing away the rubbish. I do a little 'thank you' in my mind and I smile at them. I wonder if they know I am doing this...

My first member was Opa. Now we have Oma. My gorgeous Grandma. My grandparents epitomise for me the beautiful display of traditional love. That is my opinion. When I think of Oma I think of the word 'lovely'. Throughout the whole of my life she has always called me 'lovely'. Yes Oma I am lovely; however, I got this from you. I got it from my Oma! In Stevie's song 'Isn't she lovely' he sings 'Isn't she wonderful? ..Isn't she precious?' Yes Oma, Stevie, my Oma is 'made from love.'

The next member of my family. Well members. They come as a dream team. The A-team. My cousin and her gorgeous children. My beautiful second cousins are a reflection of my incredibly brave, strong cousin who I do look at a bit in awe. I feel honoured to say we are related. They all visited me, even her children when I was in hospital. 'Big Cuz', I will always be your 'lil cuz' but actually you are more of a sister, let's be honest. I knew when I spoke to you during this tough period, even though those conversations were mainly quirky expressions and paintings of my thoughts, I knew still I was 'Uptight. Everything's alright!' Thank you for being there. I remember a book you had given Little A once talking about strong women. This definitely contributed to my inspiration of writing to the lovely young women of the world, showing every single girl is brave in her own unique way. They can be themselves.

So, the next member of my 'fam a lam'. My family squad is Dad. Yes, you know about this adventure but I can't wait for you to read this part. You always said that I should be a writer. Honestly, I never believed you until I started writing to Stevie. As you know, when I was ill I used to write pages, actually booklets of thoughts and less positive feelings. Maybe you once had a glimpse of these who knows but you knew either way that I was able to write. Dad. We had years of not really understanding each other, didn't we? Since I started writing I have seen our relationship magically blossom into that light-hearted banter and fun relationship we had when I was young. I didn't see you for the time I was in hospital. I even missed your birthday. I could not write you a card. To be honest, looking back it is because I could not face up to the truth and actually you were the one who knew me the most, you spotted the experience I had at university. You were right. 'For once in my life...' 'I can go where life leads me...somehow I know I'll be strong!' Dad, I looked at the letter you wrote me when I was absent. I promise you I will never miss another birthday of yours. You said in the letter 'no one fills the house like Ellie D'. Dad. The pea to my pod. Thank you for being there even when I wasn't. 'Love to see you...to see you love to!'

Stevie, I have spoken about my lovely parents. Anything I do, if my mum has any opinion on it I honestly value it and will 'check myself before I wreck myself' (something I ask my friends to say to me if I question something that does not need questioning) in order to ground myself. Mum is my role model but actually it is them both together that give me strength and unconditional love. So many of my amazing friends have separated families. I even have some friends who have lost a parent. However, when I look at my parents' relationship together throughout the years it has always been the foundation of what 'true, real, honest love' really is. Inspirational. You met so young but I know that when you found each other life just made sense. In Stevie's song 'You are my sunshine', I think of you both. You come as a pair. Mum isn't Mum without Dad and visa versa. A partnership of love. I have found a card that they wrote me when I finished my exams, it is a Winnie the Pooh card with the words 'We think you're a real star and we're so very, very proud of you'. The key word here being 'we'. You two are 'One'. (Ed Sheeran).

I went to Australia when I was not feeling as good as I feel now. I wanted to get away girl and see my friends who were out there. Stevie, I thought jumping on a plane, going halfway across the world would make certain less positive thoughts disappear. Little did I know my best friend, my mum would actually fly out to New Zealand, the place I left Australia to go on my own to meet me at a 'safe house' that was called 'Time Out'. I had relapsed over there, I did not look after myself away from the people I loved the most as much as I do today. Stevie, remember your family. I have just found the card my parents sent me before I went. Mum said 'I'm so very proud of you and admire what you've done and what you've become. Enjoy your trip, soak up the sun, the experiences, and the love we have for you.'

How this woman managed to write these words when she knew deep down the reality, is just incredible. She knew I wanted to go so supported my decision. Dad said, 'always thinking of you, for God's sake look after yourself. Any concerns phone straight away. Mum will be out on the first flight!' Dad, you always had the best sense of humour. I am laughing a lot right now. I hope this makes him smile and shines a little light on that experience as we look back at it now. He was right, I did call Mum. She did fly out. He brought humour to this experience for me so thank you to him. They called me 'Sunshine girl' when I was born. 'The lost years' happened but I have a feeling they are changing to the 'love years'. Thank you to writing, honesty and music I am back. Through their continuous support I am able to be the bright Sunshine girl again. Cheers guys. P.S. Mum, every appointment, every hospital visit was worth it. I promise. It got me here.

Next person. My brother. When I say that I actually laugh. My brother, no one else's. Mwahaha. He honestly makes me proud to call him my 'bro'. We have had very similar experiences in our lives. That's how I know he is my rock. He said to me last night, 'You have looked after too many people Ells'. Yes bro, I have always tried to please everyone else and in the past, I've never actually pleased myself.

I'll never forget dancing with him in the lounge to Destiny's Child, 'Independent woman'. I have an image of him jumping up behind the fluffy foot rest, singing 'question'. Little did I know back then he was encouraging me to be an independent woman. What a guy he is. He visited me in hospital and the pic 'n' mix that he brought me would make my day. Even if he did always take the last strawberry lace. Thank you for being my rock. Something our parents always gave us as kids was love. I love talking to you on a 'regular' Sunday, 'I just called to say I love you!' Speaking to him and his fiancee both on loud speaker brings me a lot of joy and comfort. Love, and thank you both.

'Higher Ground'. This tune brings me to the end of this lovely, family-filled playlist. Almost! I am going to be thanking a non blood relative. Remember the angel we spoke about a few times? This girl has appeared quite a few times in each playlist. Simple reason, I see her more as a sister than anything else. To be honest I can't thank this cherub enough. I have found a card from my twenty-second birthday from her. The card says 'fresh starts and new beginnings here we come.' And always side by side. This angel calls me an 'inspiration' for my 'strength' saying she is 'so proud'. Cherub, she is my inspiration girl. We created musicals when we were young, danced and sung our way through life to be honest, with music as the background and force of love. From songs to creating actual tickets that we would rip as my family walked into the lounge in 'The Mead' the road I live on for twenty-one years. My family would only gain entry to the musical creation and our performance if that ticket was torn as it signified VIP entry. Sister, we did Stagecoach together, ballet, school and guess what else...LIFE!

'When you believe in things you don't understand and you suffer. Superstition ain't the way!' Thank you Stevie Wonder. I have had moments in life where I have not understood certain experiences or events. Stevie. If you believe in some things that don't make you feel good, there is no reason to be 'superstitious'. I grew up feeling quite 'superstitious', however, I think we should both try flipping it. Listen to that gut of yours that is telling you something. Listen to that lovely gut and listen to a good song. Surround yourself with positive people who make you feel good. It may be family, it may be friends, a neighbour, a group, a class, or even a charity. Be with the people that support you and make you shine. Then if you want go to do a little dance or sing that song that makes you feel lovely. 'Superstition' is definitely up there for me!

Girl. Stevie. Thank you for listening to me talk about the great Mr Wonder in this playlist. I have thanked my nearest and dearest. My love for this lot has grown even more. I hope you can do the same and apply this exact same gratitude exercise to those special few in your life you see as 'family'. If you believe in the magic of life, like truly believe in it, it will appear. If you appreciate those loved ones of yours, more love will be filled into your experiences with people.

'Signed, sealed, delivered. I'm Yours.' Thank you to the great Stevie Wonder for making this such a love-filled playlist.

E. x

P.S. Remember in Stevie Wonder's words, 'If you believe in things that you don't understand.... superstition ain't the way!' ....'Isn't she lovely!' Yes girl, you are.

Putting Playlist 5 Into Practice

Independence.

If you develop independence young, I think you are more able to choose the right paths in your life but it is never too late to discover your independence. I was very dependent on my parents for so many years and heavily relied on them for reassurance and it did hold me back. I only really developed independence at the age of twenty-seven! Women especially do need to feel independent - we can't rely so much on other people especially in a romantic sense. You should always, as my Dad says, 'look out for number one!' I do that now.

Always put yourself first so you are able to help others in a much more fulfilling way. Especially when it came to my health - I lost my health and I think that really knocked my confidence in feeling independent. I was on benefits and I felt unable to contribute or be a part of society. My illnesses did knock my confidence and if I had self love from an early age I believe that I would have had a lot more years of independence. Destiny's Child "Independent Woman' comes to mind - a song my brother and I used to dance and sing to as I have previously mentioned.

As women we do now have the vote, we do now have the freedom of choice but I think we do still need sometimes guidance and we most certainly need the tools and confidence to independently say yes or no to experiences that will ultimately affect our wellbeing. The word 'no' maybe sometimes outweighing always saying 'yes'. My mum was always superstitious - which I developed. Since the book started, I have not been superstitious at all - apart from saying 'cya' instead of 'bye'. Ha. Bye feels formal. Stevie Wonder is a great example of being independent - the musical genius does not even have his vision and he has created songs that flip my mind into positivity by even the beat or tone. The lyrics are a whole other story!!

This month, think about what you've not had the confidence to do yourself or make a decision on. Write it down and put a deadline date next to it - did you know we are more likely to achieve something if we do this? Then go for it, girl! I'll be here at the finishing line #TheSunshineAdventure @eloisaroars

PL ▶ YLIST

'CAME HERE FOR LOVE'

Hello Lion, you royal thing.

'Listen to your heart above all other voices.' - Marta Kagan (Summersdale Publishers Ltd).

Girl. Ready for playlist six? I woke up today and I am writing! I just knew this playlist was going to be the best one yet. Why you ask? I just knew and believe it. I am going to have a little look back at the playlists. As you know I have spoken about themes throughout. So far in this journey of self-discovery we have realised our bravery, our honesty, our strength, our beauty, our independence. Fancy bringing a little royalty to this discovery of self-discovery? I most certainly am my girl. Let's go. Let the dancing and singing continue.

Those three words. Yes. 'I love you.' I have said them to two men. My first long term relationship and the second one a three-month 'fling'. Now, when I look back I realise it was not true, real honest love. I was quite poorly in both these experiences. I did not like myself as much as I do today. For the first one, I remember spending hours getting ready for a charity ball with my best friend at my ex-boyfriend's house. I walked in and I had to ask him if I looked okay. I burst into tears with my best friend when I went back into his room to see her. That's when I knew the relationship was not as positive as I initially thought. From being told that I ruined Valentine's day because I had three glasses of wine and because I wanted to go out and dance with him, I knew then something wasn't really clicking in my warm heart.

It is now that I write these words, I believe I was not in true, real honest love. Clothes and dancing are two expressions of who I truly am. The second 'fling' I had been involved with someone, 'The Rascal' for three months. I then started this adventure of *self-love* a week after seeing him, and realised I did not need a man to make me happy. I wanted to be happy in myself. I wanted to love me. I want to thank my ex-boyfriend for my first relationship and for ending it. I also want to thank 'The Rascal', the experience with him made me want to fall in love with myself. This playlist has been altered before I send my first draft to the publishers at Balboa Press. The reason for this Girl, is because so much has happened - meeting a certain guy and I have now developed 'self-love'. For once, I am listening to my heart and the world so it is only fair that I speak the honest truth in this playlist and tell you what got me to this point...right, Girl?

My girl, once lion cub who I believe has gained all the qualities to be that stunning, effortlessly strong lioness now, are we ready to listen to Elton John's classic 'Can you feel the love tonight?' Fabulous. I thought you may say yes. I am ready too...

So I have said Lion, you royal thing I am going to be calling you Queen in this chapter. I hope that is okay. Yes, we were all princesses once when we were younger. For me, I was a bit of a tomboy one. With a sprinkle of 'girly'. My favourite colour was pink, what was yours? There are so many beautiful colours to choose from. For me, I was a bit of a 'tomboy'. Yes, I always loved pink and pretty things and yet, any excuse to borrow my brother's hoody or wear a hat backwards and I would grab the opportunity. Although disguising sometimes behind this exterior of comfort, I loved doll's houses, dressing up in pink, and being a 'girl'. I also knew my favourite colour was pink and I wanted a prince to 'rescue' me from that tower. Well, I thought I wanted a prince. Actually little did I know then, I actually needed myself to lower me down off that castle.

Remember at the start of this playlist I called you natural. I cannot wait for you, Queen to find out why. When I was younger I always had a ' schoolgirl crush' on Prince Harry. I mean, who wouldn't? He is a prince and obviously lovely. He has a kind smile and plays rugby. He is a prince for goodness sake. I knew deep down it was more than his looks that made me like him. There was something about his voice, the way he spoke, his empathy and care that I knew was behind that lovely face of his. His mind in particular made me look at him with those puppy love eyes and say 'woah!' The reason for talking about Prince Harry as a symbol of a Lion is yes because he is royalty but I think we both know there is more to this lion than what it is in those eyes. There is a Lion or Lioness out there for everyone. Or if there isn't, then it is you anyway. That in itself is enough.

For you it may be a Lion, it may even be a Lioness. Personally for me, it is a Lion. I do have a type. Initially, I thought it was a physical type. It is actually the mind that attracts me. If someone is able to light up the world with their eyes and smile I know that they are the Lion. Their values reflect my values. Their humour reflects my humour. Don't you agree Queen? Of course, physical attraction is good but actually a personality and a sense of humour for me is better. A magnetic connection. I want to fall in love with someone's soul, not because they have a 'great bod'. I knew that when I would meet him, I would know he is the one I have been waiting for to enter my life right now. I hope you like my 'quirky' idea of what true, honest love is but I really do believe it is about the soul. A soulmate. 'Mate' being a crucial part of it, wouldn't it be great to meet someone who is also your best mate? I have a feeling there is someone out there for us all, Queen. A very lovely belief I have about this wonderful world.

Lioness, our once princess who is now a Queen. In the film 'The Lion King' Nala sings in unison with Simba when he is talking about his excitement to become King. I believe she is the driving force for him returning home. Lioness, our once princess who is now a Queen. Are you ready Queen? You were born ready. Truth. There's always magic to be found if you seek it out. Magic girl, queen, Lioness. We want magic, don't we? Are we enough for magical experiences? Yes girl, we 100% are.

Firstly, thank you so much to Prince Harry for symbolising a lovely prince. You have set up incredible mental health charities because you are a person who has recovered from your own experiences. I don't think we ever actually 'recover' as such from trauma in our life. However, you are a symbol of love. It is an honour for me to be British. My life experiences make a lot of sense now. Thank you for your grace, it is honourable. Also, thank you to 'The Rascal' that entered my life in October 2018. He is going to be mentioned in this playlist too.

I am going to be looking at the gorgeous Ella Eyre's words in this playlist. This stunning lady supported Little Mix when I saw them that day at Twickenham Stoop. I just knew I was supposed to be at that concert.

'Be yourself; everyone else is taken.' These words are from Oscar Wilde. Inspiring or what? Queen, I cannot stress that enough. In previous relationships with men if I am honest alcohol has been present a lot. Not all of them but enough to make me know I was never my real true self when alcohol was in the 'mix.' That was not a fun kind of DJ mix to the magical playlist of my mind. **You are the DJ of your mind.** I have had experiences where I look back and if I'm honest I used to panic and worry which led to more years of less self-worth or belief. More importantly, not enough self-love. When I started seeing the Rascal I was not fully appreciative of what I had in life. Then things started happening and changing. Have you ever posted a selfie or actually I will go as far as saying that I used to post pictures with so many filters it never looked like me. I was even told about this app that actually 'slims' your face. These pictures were my dating profile. When I write this, I am actually a little shocked of this truth. My dating profile and image was never me. No, I was never a 'catfish' but my image was not the real lioness.

I also used to get messages from my friends and they would say 'Ells, why did you delete that picture on Instagram? Is it because you didn't get any likes?' No, girls. My best friends. I would delete those pictures because it was not me. I actually deleted social media this week for the sole reason that I wanted to put my heart into this adventure with you, Queen. I have yes, of course, regularly spoken to my friends and family every day. Probably more than ever. I knew the questions about everything would come out when I wrote. It has! Was I truly happy? My gorgeous Queen I deeply am now and I hope you are too. My cheeks are going very red right now. They are burning with emotion and feeling again.

You can learn from your past. Those dreams have a magical meaning. Girl, Queen. When I was ill I couldn't sleep which led to years of disturbed nights. I look back now and I can see it is because I was not being my true, honest self. I was in disguise with how I really felt about the world. I am now proud of who I am. I have learnt to spend time with people who truly love me for me, the real Lioness. No matter what has happened prior to now. We are feeling love, so let's shout 'love, love, love!' Thank you to my heart for being able to feel honest love. You are ace. So is yours, Queen. Give your heart a massive cuddle. Hello self-love. I am playing 'Comeback' by Ella Eyre. A song with a touch of loveliness. The love comeback is definitely stronger than that lost setback, right? This song really helped me recently. We have all been hurt but it is a case of coming back stronger and letting that pain burn. Thank you Ella Eyre.

Okay, so I met the Rascal before I beganwriting this journey. We met in a pub near me. We spoke for a whole month before we met again. In the past, I had never done this. I would usually meet men after a day or two, maybe a week if I was 'lucky' before I met them in person. A 'good vibe' and energy I got from his pictures and the way he interacted with me. I thought he was genuine. It felt effortless. Even an emoji made me smile. I am quite simple at heart. My real self was starting to shine through. I was becoming aware of who I really was and what I wanted.

He felt like a friend. I thought I could be honest and open with him. A friend who I knew I was going to 'fancy'. Before we met I even said to him, 'I am a bit worried'. He asked 'why?' He knew why. He said to me one night on the phone 'you are so easy to talk to. I haven't even spoken to a girlfriend like this on the phone before.' My first thought was 'yeah right'. He must be a player. He screenshotted a conversation we had once and sent it to me. I noticed he had not saved my number. I also noticed in the top right-hand screen he had the dating profile on in the background. Remember that lovely gut I told you to listen to? Hello, you gorgeous gut.

Yeah, I was pretty observant! Whoops. He was on Bumble when we were matched and was on it whilst he was talking to me? Hm. I felt suspicious to be honest. I was like 'Ellie, he is a player'. We had a couple of weeks of 'fun' and 'light-hearted' experiences. When I hear the song 'Ego' by Ella Eyre I say 'hello you.' This is exactly how I felt about this Rascal that was stood in front of me when we met. 'I see you looking in the mirror...I see you thinking that you're killer' I did actually feel like one of many. That is how I felt. In the screenshot, there was also around sixteen unread conversations. Yep they may have been friends but at the back of my head I was thinking, 'all women Ellie, all women. Run away.' 'If I got under the surface. I wonder if you'd even notice'. I wanted a Lion without an ego.

However, girl…Queen. I knew it was not the Rascal making me feel like this. I had created this 'image' of what I thought he was and I believe it was mirrored back to me. 'Don't let it go blow up your ego!' I used to always resist at the beginning saying how 'good looking' I thought he was because I didn't want to 'boost his ego'.

Initially, I did think this. 'I see you acting like you're modest…' To be honest when I look back at this experience I felt like I was doing things for him. Every message, every picture, even gift was for him. It was never for myself. I never had self-love or appreciation. I even sent him a Valentine's card with a pillow mist to help him sleep and a copy of 'The Secret'. I needed to give myself sleep and gratitude! The reality was I got nothing back. I never expected anything, I genuinely didn't but it still didn't make me feel great; little did I know I was about to give him a lot more…those three words.

We spent a lot of Sundays together. Pretty much every Sunday he would be at mine. I did have in this head of mine that he was a player. That is the truth. That is what I told myself so it had to be true, right? I had a previous relationship as I have mentioned where trust was broken. I was actually slightly alien from the person I had been with for almost two years because I thought that relationship was built on stability. The relationship was not as real as I hoped. This similarly encouraged me towards feelings of wanting self-love, although I did not know how to explore this yet. I told 'The Rascal' he restored my faith in men. I thought he had. I did tell him this once but I think he may not have quite believed me. I'm not surprised, I didn't actually believe me. It wasn't real. From a girl who was called the 'ice queen' by previous men to now being called 'pretty' by the Rascal. I wasn't sure how to process this all. It didn't feel like the real values I was brought up with.

The experiences began as a physical attraction. When I hear 'Answerphone' I think of Newcastle. He went there when we had only met a couple of times. As I type this up I am actually laughing. **This is shining a light.** He went there to see some friends. Something was telling me he was seeing a girl. Whether or not he did, I don't know but it doesn't actually matter. My gut was definitely shouting at me at this point, end it. At the start of seeing this guy I did actually end it. I said I was looking for more than a bit of fun and he told me he was not in a position to have a relationship with me. A few weeks later this changed and we continued to see each other. I knew deep down that he wasn't my real life Lion but I wanted to try and 'control' how he felt about me. I thought I wanted reassurance. Actually, I wanted *self-love*.

When he was in Newcastle I was with two friends telling them how much I didn't trust him. Not trusting him actually fuelled my mind into more thoughts of not trusting this guy. Naturally, friends do support what you say and feel. They encouraged me to call him. Yes, I spoke to his answerphone! 'I got a feeling. I'm overthinking 'bout thinking, you're thinking of leaving.' My thoughts were being validated. I was searching for evidence and I got it. He didn't pick up. He doesn't like me? Blah. I have memories of seeing this guy and I felt like he always wanted to leave. He would only be at mine for maybe three hours if I was 'lucky'. I don't blame him but I do understand now what he means when he said we had 'no electricity' between us. I will never forget those 'yawns' I would be greeted to on a Sunday evening. Or the rapid exits out of my flat from him. My gut always knew but I did not have enough self-love to realise it was never about me, it was about him. He wanted his Lioness. I knew I deserved a Lion.

After a few more times we met, I remember he was in my flat and I checked his bumble location. Why? I honestly think it is because I knew the only way for me to get close to him I needed to validate why I didn't trust him. He left my flat and I noticed his location was the same location as mine. He used the app in my flat. I messaged him having a go at him saying 'you were on Bumble in my flat!' His reply. No, I wasn't. Whether or not he was or wasn't it really doesn't matter. The fact that I had to check his location on the dating profile we had met on showed me that I never trusted him. I had not reached self-love or worth yet. I repeatedly asked him if we could go for dinner, I even would say 'let's go for a drink'. I would say this to encourage myself that I was more than just 'my body'. I asked him if we could go for dinner a lot and he never wanted to. We clearly did not have the same intentions or values from the get go. He was not my mirror.

On the 24th January, I started doing this 'gratitude practice' on the relationship I had with him. I wanted to make sense of what had happened between us. I wanted answers to show me that I was able to love someone. I wrote down the practice I wanted to change a relationship into 'love.' By writing these words on my paper I actually meant for myself. *Self Love.* He gave me confidence. Actually, he gave me the confidence to want self-love, not love from him.

I read my first book for the first time in six years when I started talking to the Rascal. After reading 'The Secret' by Rhonda Byrne, I then read 'Magic'. I found a book that I connected to. Maybe it was then that I knew it would be an experience that would shape me into the best person I am today. I remember him messaging me when I didn't reply like, 'I am more interesting than reading' something along those words. Our interests and values were different. I told him about this adventure. He says he 'didn't mind' but actually I do. When I finished this adventure I sent him about ten messages and tried to call him. He never replied. I text him in the morning apologising but actually for me that was another sign of my gut, this book has happened because the experience has taught me to love myself.

Okay, Queen. As you know this playlist has been changed before submitting my final draft. Initially, I did talk about how I thought I 'loved him'. I never did. It was an 'imaginary' kind of love. I had not seen him for six weeks but I wrote down a list of values I would want in my real life Lion, **the main thing I value being honesty.** Honesty has made this adventure even better so here we go. Just over a week ago we had quite a deep conversation. We were going back and forth. We actually had our first 'argument'. I say argument but to me it actually felt like we were doing a bit of 'real talk' that Ella Eyre sings about. When I first met him I did say after a few times we met that we were looking for different things. I wanted more and I knew he wasn't in a position to give me that. He said at the start he was not in a position to commit to a relationship with someone. Despite this, I did say to him I was happy to carry on seeing him. I said to myself 'even if he is in your life that is better than not having him at all'. Actually looking back, it is better to not have someone in your life than a kind of relationship where you do not feel 'enough'. Something I never realised until I started writing to you.

'That day' we had a conversation. I even said to him on the phone, 'I don't want a relationship!' I knew deep down that my relationship was actually with this adventure with you and then I would be ready to meet my Lion. These words and experiences I've shared with you have come from my honest heart. It was the only way for me to express what my life had been about. It was an adventure I wanted to take to explain why self-love is so important to our lovely creative minds and hearts. That day, I will never forget it. I then said to him I do want a relationship. I always did, I think he always deep down knew. I did want a relationship with him.

Prior to this I had written him a four-page letter which pretty much said everything I felt. It was the most emotive letter I have ever written. I also included a letter I had received from my dad when I was in hospital. Once I told him that I did want a relationship with him, he said he did not feel the 'electricity' between us. Deep down, I knew exactly why. He was right. The person I actually wanted to fall in love with was myself. For once, I wanted to love myself. It was time to feel good about myself and what I had **achieved.**

After hearing the words 'no electricity', I said exactly how I felt. It took me about fifty minutes to compose that message to him. It wasn't easy. I said in the message I would rather he did not reply then message me something like you always say 'go find someone else who can give you a relationship' or 'good luck with the book'. I started this adventure a week after I saw him. A week later I began writing about self-love.

So 'that night' if I'm honest Queen, I did not sleep. I woke up the next day and I wasn't sure how much sleep I had got. It was a pretty disturbed night. Why? I hadn't been fully honest with him. I thought I loved him and he had no idea how I felt. So yes, I wrote that message and told him how I felt. I got no reply. Weirdly that did not make me sad. What did make me feel less positive was that I sent him 'that letter'. 'That letter' which pretty much had my heart in it from my Dad. I sent it and heard nothing. No one had seen this letter other than my dad. I messaged him on the Sunday saying 'Did you get my letter?' He replied 'Yes, I did thanks.' I said 'Good.' No reply after that.

I saw two of my best friends today. Remember my 'Leigh Anne'? I told them what had happened and about my dad's letter. They spoke to me today and I knew deep down I deserved a message from him. A message at least just to say something. Anything. Even an emoji.

However, a week had gone by and I had received nothing from him. I messaged him and said I wasn't sure I could really understand why he had not acknowledged my letter or my dad's letter. For me, it wasn't so much my letter, it was my dad's one that made **my stomach go into knots** when he had not even mentioned it. I had put in a picture of me and my brother when we were younger so he could see the Sunshine Girl for who she really was. He said he had acknowledged it. That was literally all he said. For me. That was enough.

Enough to know that yes, the experiences with him did teach me honest love. It taught me honest love for myself. I realise now that I am 100% enough as I am. I recently have been listening to Marisa Peer and Louise Hay. Queen, you should totally look these inspirational women up. Marisa's three words 'you are enough' and Louise's life changing affirmations 'I approve of myself'. I will be saying these words every day for as long as I am here now. I listened to one video on Louise Hay about Self-Love after I wrote the book. I wrote an affirmation 'I approve of myself' on my hand' and it stayed on my hand over night. That is when I knew in my soul that I had a gift to help young women. I listen to her most days now.

The relationship in this chapter has taught me that I can be honest, I can love and I can love myself. Actually, my feelings towards him were more of an 'imaginary' love. Would I really want to be with someone who does not acknowledge that huge part of my life through my Dad's words? I know deep down it isn't. I want someone who is going to see that letter and call me. I no longer want or have to chase after men (butterflies) to get reassurance. He sent me one other message saying he had nothing else to say. That line will stay with me as I write these words. It explains that our values are actually different. Honesty has meant that Queen, I can show you honest love is actually better first done on yourself than with someone you spend a few hours with on a Sunday.

Queen. I have not seen The Rascal since this journey began. The real magic did not happen because of him. It happened because of me. It happened because of us. Love yourself and then everything will start to fall into place. Do you know what girl? I am very excited for the real life Lion. We all have a Lion or Lioness. Not an imaginary kind of love but a real love that is out there. Exciting or what!

Thank you to Prince Harry for being such a lovely, honourable, contemporary representation of today's world and awareness of mental health. Thank you to the Rascal. You showed me that honest love can exist for yourself if you believe in it and it has meant that I now understand self-love.

I found a quote today on Pinterest and Google, it said 'World population: 7,810,423,756. Just in case someone's acting irreplaceable. Remember that one, Girl. If you can be pretty and natural to someone, I'm sure you can be that to so many people. 'We don't have to take our clothes off to have a good time'. Well said, Ella Eyre! Thank you so much for your real, royal music. Be yourself, Queen! See ya in the next playlist, gorgeous Lioness.

E. x

P.S. Lion, I am ready for you now. Are you? Send me your 'Location' - Burna Boy/Dave.

Putting Playlist 6 Into Practice

Royalty.

In this chapter, I hoped you felt royal. A Queen. 'Yas Queen!' Comes to mind....I think that if the reader sees themselves as their own version of a Queen then they will treat themselves with respect, care, and worthiness. The theme of this chapter is really to be yourself. Every experience I have had that has not made me feel good has come down to the fact that I have not been myself with these men or even friends. I was always trying to please other people - forgetting to please myself. I needed to put myself first. For once. Since the book started, I have done nothing but love and respect who I am which has meant my world has totally changed. I do want you in this chapter to be able to look at your past in the way I have. To shine a light on every experience so you can create a magical future.

Self-love is very much a theme and teaching of this chapter too - and to be honest throughout! I find Ella Eyre's lyrics perfect because she does 'dig a little deeper' and talk about love in a way that is very relatable and contemporary, for example 'Answerphone'.

The reason I mentioned the song 'Location' song above is because I recently heard this and when I put it on my whole body felt calm. It made sense as to why it has so much meaning to me. In a past relationship, I was told at the end 'by the way every time you thought I was in my flat gaming, I wasn't. I was at the pub'. My gut flipped at this time telling me I should have listened. When I was ill I just wanted the ones I loved with me. In the ward, or on those nights out where I did not know where I was I wanted them to know my location. I have a memory living in London standing at a bus stop terrified, calling my mum because a night had gone badly with a man. They picked me up. I wanted to find someone who I could call when I needed them and they would be straight there. I always wanted people to know my location and I wanted to know they would be there straight away.

When I wrote this book I wrote a little note on my phone of the ideal 'Lion' that would exist for me. I truly believe if you believe in something enough it will manifest into your reality. So grab a pen and write your version of your own Lion. You don't need to share this one but keep it close. I have a second challenge for you that I'd love for you to share! A queen will always walk tall and with confidence so relax your shoulders, straighten your posture, and hold your head high. Next time you are out of the house, walk like a queen for the day.

Share a selfie of you when you feel most queen-like #TheSunshineAdventure @eloisaroars

PL⏵YLIST

MY PLAYLIST

Hello Eloisa, you free thing. Stop chasing those butterflies. Chase yourself!

'There is no greater thing you can do with your life and your work than follow your passions' - Richard Branson (Summersdale Publishers Ltd).

Hello gorgeous reader. What a special adventure we have been on so far. I don't know about you but I am definitely feeling a little 'jazzy'. I have a lovely friend with a name like this. I'm feeling 'self-lovey'. I have not written in two days now because honestly I knew magic was going to appear before my sparkly eyes. My gosh, it has girl. In this chapter, I am going to call you girl again. I hope that is okay. The reason for this is because initially that is how this adventure began. It also reminds me of my youth which makes me smile.

In this chapter, I am solely talking about my experiences. As you know, I had my first panic attack when I was sixteen and I was still having them up until I started this journey with you. I want to go through what I believe has truly made me better. I had a feeling today would be the day I told you. I have just come back from therapy and I knew I was ready to start this chapter. Girl, I was discharged from my therapist. My gosh, I cannot wait to explain why and how I have got to this. Want to take a walk on the wild side and hear how I got to this moment? Great. I was glad to hear that virtual nod. Sending you a virtual sunshine cuddle back. May this begin...

I'll paint you a picture. I was fortunate to attend great schools. I am so grateful and thankful to my parents for giving me that great education I was able to get. Education really is special. Thank you to my parents for putting me through fantastic schools where I not only met friends for life I developed an education which shaped my life. The girls' school I went to is shouting at me as I write this. Whether it is pick 'n' mix sweets from Tesco, the lyrics of Mitchell Brothers, the film Kidulthood or that famous night at one of my friends. The night which we thought was actually a 'Skin's party'. A show we all religiously watched at the time of the school days where sixteenth birthdays were pretty much our necessity. Who had kissed who was the main focus of much of our daily lives. We would thrive off who had their first kiss. Or their first dance. It was exciting. It was youthful. It was our life.

By the way, girl. Before I started this playlist, it was Valentine's Day. It was the best Valentine's of my life. I promise you that. I went to a healing sanctuary with my dear mum where I had been before with friends. I have connected to the sanctuary a lot. I go there and I feel real. It gives me clarity and I connect with Opa. Before I went there, I had no idea I was a spiritual kind of girl or what to expect. I went there and discovered my heart and mind were connected. Something I never knew were even linked. I connected with Opa that day and started writing this adventure that evening. It is clear to see that I see that lovely haven as a source of much inspiration. Thank you to the sanctuary, Harry Edwards!

So I am writing this part to you on a Friday night. If someone had told me ten years ago I would be writing a book on a Friday night I probably would have laughed. I would probably try to say something back with 'wit'. Yet, here I am. Do you know what, girl? As each words goes onto the page I am getting happier and happier. I said I would paint you a picture. So I am sitting here. With a jumper on that I bought this week. I bought it for what I thought I would wear for a Lion on my first date.

Last night, I was totally convinced that guy I just spoke about would rock up to mine with flowers. He didn't. Was I disappointed? Of course. Initially. Then I stepped back and looked at myself in the mirror with this jumper on and I thought wow. I looked really pretty. It is a long sleeve white jumper with a high neck and has a floral print on it. Something I've never felt until I realised I was actually buying this jumper for myself. That felt really good girl. Real good. A sparkly kind of **'electricity'** good. Get my vibe? I remember in the past I would buy outfits I thought men would like. Actually, it was never me. It was a facade to appear 'sexy'.

Okay. I am also sitting here with gorgeous nails. That might sound strange but I have never had nails. I had them once and that was when I was in Paris for six weeks on an internship. I loved Paris and I felt happy there. It was romantic. I also wanted to go there one day with a prince. Actually, I did go. By myself, aged around twenty. Six weeks. I loved it. My gorgeous friends visited me there. School friends, a Stagecoach beauty, and university friends. Some may say I am quite a popular girl! Something I never realised when I was ill. I thought I lost every friend but I hadn't. They were always there, even if my mind wasn't.

My aim for this playlist is yes to talk through my experiences. I will be sharing with you my favourite tunes that I grew up listening to which have shaped who I am today and why I think music is very powerful. It is magical. I will talk a bit through my life to explain what has helped me. Everyone is different and that is what makes us all so special and unique. My therapist said she wanted to work in partnership with me one day. She is one incredible woman. My gosh she has got me to this place of real self-belief. As I write this, I realise that it was never the previous man that gave me self-belief it was her. Yes, he gave me huge confidence and belief in myself that I was worthy to be talking to him. Actually, the real self-belief happened that day I stepped into my therapist's lounge. I opened up to her. This angel made me believe in myself. I have a feeling we are going to be revealing a bit more of why this book came about.

As I write this I am listening to my favourite songs. I woke up yesterday and I was feeling so much love. Yes, love from the previous chapters I have shared with you. Also, love for myself. **Self-love.** I actually said to myself this year that my New Year's resolution would be 'Self-love.' I had never truly known what it meant. However, I knew I wanted to learn about it. I wanted to study it. I wanted to hear stories about it. I wanted to believe in it. I wanted to practice it. I wanted to share it with you Queen. I had no idea making that resolution last month that a flipping book would be made about self-belief which equated into self-love.

So the first song I have on is Little Bow Wow featuring Jojo. I know the girls from secondary school will probably 'howl' with laughter when they hear this. I am howling too, I promise. I loved Bow Wow at school. Yes, girls you can say those words, 'she cried at school because she wanted to be Jojo. She was crying because she wanted to be Little Bow Wow's girl.' I always loved R'n'B and hip hop. Thanks to my brother, I grew up listening to all those 'Slow Jams'. Thank you Twista! In Bow Wow and Jojo's song, 'Baby it's you', I wanted someone to sing this about me! It is me that has got me here though. 'If I'm witchu I'll be alright!' Yes, Bow Wow I have always adored your music. You were my school crush. I always loved your music. I still do. Although, I have now realised I love me. I never thought I'd apply your beautiful lyrics to lyrics about myself. Hehe.

I grew up loving hip hop. There was something about the genre I was drawn to. Those beats did things to my body and heart that made me want to dance. Every song felt very real and I just felt good growing up to it. From favourites of Wayne Wonder, Fabolous, Chingy, Kano, Jagged edge and Ginuwine 'Ugh'! I'm listening to 'Differences' by Ginuwine now and it makes me feel so good. 'You are so sweet, no one competes'. Wow Ginuwine. I will share with you a few songs from my own 'youth' playlist:

'Miss Independent' - Neyo
Differences - 'Ginuwine'
'Bounce Along' / 'No letting go' - Wayne Wonder
'This is the girl' - Kano
'One Call Away' - Chingy
'Walked Outta Heaven' / 'Let's get Married' - Jagged Edge
'Into you' / 'Can't let you go' - Fabolous
'My Baby' - Lil Bow Wow/Jagged Edge
'Cater to you' - Destiny's Child
Survivor - Destiny's Child
'No games' - Serani

Girl, the reason for sharing these select songs with you are simple. They make me happy. They remind me of my youth. Whatever you are listening to in your teens, remember these songs. No matter what you grew up listening to, popping your little head to. Enjoy these songs. Tilt your crown and remember them. Feel them. Appreciate them. Sing if you want to. Dance if you want to. This reminds me of the song by Dua Lipa 'Want to'. A song, I believe is to put it simply, the future. Any song I chose, I apply it to my life and it makes sense for me as I get older. I was blessed to go to a Destiny's Child concert with a lovely school friend when I was younger. Destiny's Child do make me happy. They obviously epitomise strong, independent women which I love. Do you agree? I'm listening to 'Girl' and I love it. So I'm going to listen to it to continue this feeling of happy thoughts. That is the aim of this adventure. To feel good. Thank you, Destiny's Child! 'Dance for you' by Beyoncé is featuring too. Welcoming yours truly. You. Queen.

Okay. I am feeling good. I hope you are too. Let's continue! I don't know if you know the artist Aaliyah. There is a song of hers called 'Miss You'. I have memories of listening to this in my study in The Mead. Thinking of my Opa. A lot of tears were shed during this period. I have never felt so connected to him as I do right now. I have a picture of him in a frame here with me now with candles. 'What am I gonna do?' 'I want to cry some time.' Yes Opa, I miss him dearly. We all do. However, he never really went. We lost him that day. Yes, I am welling up because he knew it was a wonderful world even if he was not with us. I am listening to it now and I am crying. Really good tears girl. 'Skies are blue' 'clouds are white'.

Yes, Opa I do now think to myself 'what a wonderful world'. As I write this, I am smiling, smiling not just for him but for myself and the wonderful world that we live in. I am wonderful, you are wonderful Nala. Thank you to Opa for leaving this song for us to remind us how wonderful the world really is if you believe it is. I am going to put on a song now because I want that heartbreak to go to a heart-up. The song I chose was 'Old Town Road' - Lil Nas X featuring Billy Ray Cyrus. Queen, I will always put this on now when I think of my Dear Opa. Heart-up complete. Tick.

Girl, I have just popped Marques Houston on. 'Clubbin' I just had one of my favourite meals. Carbonara. I am definitely smiling girl. So as you know my panic attacks started at school. Little did I know then in a few years later I would be admitted into hospital for psychosis. Ready girl for some 'real talk'. I know I am. We were born ready. I have a feeling this will be an interesting little playlist. Ready to feel me set free? I will be doing this in the most honest way as possible to give you that little bit of hope and belief. No matter what you are going through. You can set yourself free. Be honest with yourself. Then the world is your rainbow. You are the pot of gold at the end. By the way girl, I have my playlist on and I promise you I feel really good as I write this. I actually know most of the words to every song.

I went to university after sixth form and my world changed. From that smiley, happy, bubbly popular Sunshine girl. I was about to enter into a six-year experience of something less positive. Health less good than it was before. Girl, I want to tell you this to bring a lot of realism to this playlist. Through our connection I have become brave. You have helped me be honest, given me strength, seen my inner beauty and independence. You have made me feel **royal.** Even so, things are about to get even better. I am going to be set free from my past. The only way to do this it to look at it. Face it. Hello Fear. I am ready for you now. Roar. Let us have a little chat. I will be honest about it and feel gratitude for it. It has made me who I am. Mum, you always said I was 'special' I believe you now. Queen, you are special too I promise you that.

Before I say what I do I need to thank a few people first. Obviously my family. Without you, I'm not sure I would be able to write these words. My friends, without you all I would not have been so strong over the years. Although I was absent from you all, you I never left. In particular, one of my best friends, she knows who she is. You visited me in hospital. I love you and I promise you I am back for good now. I will be there until we are old and grey discussing Harry Potter, singing to 'Dear Diary'. Thank you to my incredible therapists. Two women in particular. The one I saw when I had my first panic attack, you were so kind and lovely. You knew when I saw you again a few years later you could not help me. I needed a doctor. Thank you to the angel I met last year who I have already mentioned. You made me feel at ease the minute I stepped into your lovely lounge. There was something about those candles and your voice that relaxed me. I trusted you. I knew honesty was going to make me better, and it did.

Thank you to the Lion I am with now for entering my life just before the book is published, now confident but still learning. I can feel my real, quirky self with him. After talking about 'psycho.NO.sis', his response made me think 'yeah he has a cool mind'. I never have to worry about his location and I know if I send him my location he will be straight there. Psycho.no.bro. Cheers to the 'Good life', Kanye West.

Girl. I am listening to a song that I used to play at University. I played it on repeat when I was ill. I remember locking myself in my room listening to this all the time. I want to take myself there because I want to show you no matter how life gets there is a way from a less dark life to a very positive one. A one with light and stars. When I first went to university there was someone there that I knew before. Little did I know then that I was about to fall into six years of something described as the opposite to a dream. Looking back now it was a beautiful little nightmare that led me here to you.

The relationship with him was not a relationship, it wasn't even a case of 'seeing each other'. It was something I can describe as an 'agreement'. An agreement I made with myself to have a lot to drink to get confidence to try and 'impress' him.

It was a guy I thought I trusted but ultimately it was an 'agreement' that I didn't talk to anyone about. I didn't even tell my family about it, or my friends. I was ashamed. I felt guilty which affected me for years. Hiding something really can affect your wellbeing. Something small or big. We didn't see much of each other but it did become a somewhat infatuation where I wanted to constantly prove to him I was worthy of his company. As you can probably guess this took a toll on my health.

I will not be sharing this song with you because I want this to be a happy experience for you. It is a great song but my interpretation of it is when I wasn't in the best place. It is **association**. A bit like when I was dating someone and he said 'woah you're having a lot of sauce with your fajitas' which led to seven years of hardly touching ketchup. I actually associate eating ketchup as the 'pain' experience. Do not change for anyone Queen. Eat the ketchup!

If I had heard the university song now without having those experiences I know I would love it. I played this song with the Lion and it has shone a huge light on those dark experiences for me. I had a night with the man at university that didn't make me feel good about myself. I thought he was really good looking. A good-looking kind of 'bad' boy. Whenever I saw this guy, I never felt myself. I did not feel as worthy as I feel today. I was a little bit scared to be a woman. A little worried to be feminine. I did not feel safe being myself and ladylike.

This 'agreement' and 'secret' I kept to myself caused me feelings of guilt because I knew people had got together with him that I knew. I felt so guilty during this period. To me this experience felt like a 'secret'. A secret I did not like. I have asked my friends today about how I was when I spoke about him or when they saw me with him or what I perceived as 'chasing' him. A 'bad guy' kind of butterfly. The words that these girls have used will stay with me forever. 'It was like you were doing something you shouldn't.' This one in particular shows why I was not happy during this period. I was not being honest. One went as far as saying it was 'abusive'. However, I have little memories of the experiences with him so these are not my words.

Honesty has always been a part of me. The experiences that happened over that six-year period, honesty was never there. I would lie to people about what I had been through, I would lie more importantly to myself about how I felt. I actually do not have any bad feelings towards this person. If anything, I am thankful to these experiences. We were never in a relationship. To me, it did not feel like a happy drug. I remember him saying within the last year, we should meet to help with my body confidence. Experiences with this person knocked my confidence. Truth. I would probably laugh and try and make 'light' of it. The reality was, I starting to lose my mind and health. Not a fault of his. It was just the situation and how I had little self-love.

Girl, at university I did lose my way. I remember seeing him last year and he said that I had gone off the radar a bit after university. He was right, I had. I ran away from who I really was. At university, I was drinking too much. I would drink to 'escape' from what I was feeling about myself. Less confidence than I have now. I did have another experience which did detach me from this wonderful world. This meant I had several experiences I didn't enjoy for a six-year period as you know Queen. Thank you to the three girls at University in particular. You know who you are. Cubed comes to mind because we all four of us had the same name and also a feeling of 'Pebbles'.

This name 'Pebbles' was from a special Spanish senorita who gave me a lot of strength. This beautiful woman wrote me a poem called 'You and I'. It stayed with me by my bed for the past seven years. One of the 'cubed' girls called me in hospital. What a babe. The other a postcard from Guatemala. You are all such lovely, strong women. Thank you for being incredible at a very tough point of my life.

Woah. Okay, Girl. There was a lot of honesty in this playlist, wasn't there? I have quickly changed the song! Remember that song I told you to imagine in the Introduction? Do you want to know a little secret? Let's change that less light secret into a shiny bright one. Mine was 'Body' by Loud Luxury. I started seeing my therapist around September 2018. I have had years of different kinds of therapy. I was even put on a therapy programme for a diagnosis that I later discovered by receiving a letter from the psychiatrist that I had been 'misdiagnosed'. Initially, I felt let down by this because I would wake up every morning believing I had this diagnosis.

However, this psychiatrist soon discharged me, so I am thankful for that. Later, when I met this pretty, blonde wholesome therapist, I knew then my life would change. Yes, I have had six months of a lot of tears but ever since I met this teacher, psychologist, doctor, friend my world has flipped into happiness. I now 'bounce along' (Wayne Wonder) to life! One of my first hotmail addresses was 'bubbles aka bounce. Bubbles from 'The Powerpuff Girls' and 'bounce' because this was the nickname I gave myself. My friends called me Ells or Dotty B despite this attempt but that just goes to show others see you in a different way than you view yourself! Call it magic.

I was blessed to be recommended this therapist through my family. I look back at my old Instagram and I posted a video in September driving to Sussex to see my family with this song 'Body' on in the car with my friends. I recorded a video looking out the world with blue skies and a lot of green. Nature. It was a pretty video. The caption said 'leaving it all behind (insert love heart eyes emoji!)'. A couple of months later, I have created this magical adventure with you girl. My therapist has a 'holistic' approach with her patients. What a gift this woman has. She specialises in so much. I pretty much ticked every box at some point in my life. Girl, I have a tattoo on my arm that says 'Butterfly fly away'. I never knew what it meant. I would always make up stories and excuses for it to hide it. My lovely therapist said to me, maybe it is something to do with flying away from relationships or experiences. Something I used to believe was a 'scar' because I would draw butterflies in hospital and I imagined myself flying away from them. Symbolically, I always chased people when I was ill. Something I vow to never do again.

Thank you to my therapist, Doctor. I said I wanted you to be at my wedding. I meant that. My self-belief and happiness has come from all those sessions with you. I am rolling up my sleeve now looking at my tattoo. Yes, I believe it is the lyrics of the beautiful, stunning Miley Cyrus! Wow. I had never heard her song before or if I had I never realised. I remember a woman at the leisure centre where I used to work said 'That's Miley Cyrus lyrics'. I was genuinely like 'Huh!?'. What I do know now is that I am being set free from my past. From a past which has been once seen as a less positive experience to a very positive dream come true. So yes that does make perfect sense! Thank you, Miley Cyrus. You beautiful, free soul. I watched Hannah Montana. I think this woman is a symbol of pure, honest love for the world.

All this chasing away butterflies has made me feel like I want to do a bit of an identity alteration. Are you with me Queen? I like the Jungle, can you tell? Shall we call it growth? Maybe we could change chasing butterflies to becoming a true, real life Lioness. I kind of want to 'roar' in the next chapter with you. Just a little heads up. The next chapter is on you. Saving the best until last, of course. I now look at my past in amazement. It is because of this adventure that this has happened. I cannot thank you enough Queen for tuning in.

I once got hit by a bicycle when I was in London. I remember waking up on the side of the road with a fireman holding my head on that curb, I looked up and he said to me 'do not move'. I still managed to recite my brother's mobile number to the ambulance staff. There was a reason I was supposed to stay in this gorgeous world, Queen. That was so I could write to you. Help you reach self-belief and self-love. Through absolute honesty I have been set free from my past. I am happy now and I know you reaching this here with me too. Yes, it can be a challenging process to be honest with yourself but actually it is a really good, fun kind of beautiful enlightenment.

'Life is a great big canvas, and you should throw all the paint on it you can' - Danny Kaye. I have found why I am here. I cannot wait for you to find out why you are too. As Miley sings about so beautifully 'I promise you there will come a day. Butterfly fly away.'

See ya in the next chapter my girl!

E. x

P.s. I am playing 'Jungle' by Tash Sultana. You should totally pop this song on too, Queen. The story behind this woman amazes me. I believe she had Psychosis too and she has smashed it with this song in my opinion. 'Welcome to the jungle. Are you going to dance with me?' We are dancing Queen, right?

Putting Playlist 7 Into Practice

All the qualities and themes that have been mentioned in the book have meant that I have been set 'free' from pain. Butterfly Fly Away is on my arm and I never knew the meaning until I met my therapist and wrote this book. Spooky. Hey! Nope. Spiritual and lovely. I no longer chase butterflies. I roar.

The songs I have added are a combination of a few of my favourite songs when I was young so I am able to relate to the reader at their age - to show that we are tuned into when we are young we will not forget - they makes us who we are. I still love all of those tunes!

Teaching is to believe in your magical dreams, follow your passion - even if you do not know what it is yet, write down a list of your hobbies or ones you'd love to try this year or next - simple but effective. 'Things that make me feel like sunshine' or something. I think the more simple it is - the better. You could even make this into a vision board!

I'd love to see what you come up with #TheSunshineAdventure @eloisaroars

PL▶YLIST
8

YOUR PLAYLIST

Hello sunshine Lioness, you special thing.

'Every moment starts a new page in your story. Make it a great one today.' - Doe Zantamata. (Summersdale Publishers Ltd).

Hello you. What a magical adventure we have had. Am I right? You are right. I woke up super early today, at 5.30am. I feel great. I knew that was a cue from the Universe and world that I needed to start the wonderful chapter on your special self. Yep. You. This book is your book. It was designed for you. This journey of self-discovery would not have happened without you, Queen.

Initially, I thought men had given me self-belief. You gave me this gift. I cannot thank you enough. Now, it is my time to return the lovely favour. This chapter is all about you. Every thought, every feeling, it is going to be coming from you and I want you to be able to apply it all to your lovely life now, today, tomorrow, and every day for the rest of your magical life.

Of course, I am here with you. And yet, I am sensing you are realising your inner 'goddess'. Your inner potential to shine that little bit more than you already do. Although I get a 'vibe' and energy that you already do this without even realising. You were drawn to this book for a reason. My aim is to be here for you. You began this journey as a soft, pretty, natural cub and my aim at the end of this playlist is for you to 'roar.' We will roar together. Tiny lionesses roar the loudest, girl. You ready?

So the reason for spending more time on this one is because this journey has been structured daily on the basis of the magic that has been happening before my eyes. I have come straight back and told you every experience which has naturally formed this magical adventure. Little did I know, this was all happening because of the presence of you in my life.

Whatever age you are reading this at, I believe you saw the magical three words 'music' 'thoughts' and 'lioness' and gravitated to this book. Whether it be the front cover, the back of the book or the font. It may have even been the picture. It could have been the word 'playlist'. Whichever it is, you were drawn to this book. It was your choice, it is actually you, that has made this adventure happen. Thank you to you my lovely reader. You. 'Inserts love heart emoji and cuddle emoji!'

Before we get going on this special, gifted subject of you. I would like to share a song with you. One of my friend's sister introduced me to it. I was like 'ugh!'. 'Ugh' meaning wow! I love this song, the tune. Yes. The artist singing. Yes. The beat. Yes. I just knew when I heard it there was more to it than this. Now I know why. I think back to the last relationship I spoke to you about. 'Hope', The Chainsmokers. It is a beautiful song and I hope if you ever do not feel like you are enough for someone, you listen to this and know that is is never about you. You are beautiful and enough exactly as you are. Never change for anyone.

This song for me relates to that relationship. Surprisingly, also every other relationship I had after I was involved in that relationship until I met the Lion. This paragraph was changed when I typed up this adventure ready to send it to the publisher. I was not ready to face up to this realisation. I am so ready to face it now girl, do you know why? Those relationships were never honest, real love. They were hope.

I hear this song now and I am really smiling. With reference to one of the relationships I spoke about, I said to this one guy that I was back on a dating site, I thanked him for a really fun couple of months and I said 'go find your girl'! I am always here as a friend. I did not get a reply. So I really hope he finds what he is looking for.

More importantly, I met a Lion. There is a Lion out there I believe for everyone. Or another Lioness. Whichever you want. For me, it is very much the Lion that came and met me at Clapham Junction on that hot summer's day. I wrote the following words down before I met him. 'I know I will know when I see him. I bet he is so lovely. I bet he reflects who I am, the most important thing to me. I believe he will reflect my values. Hello King.'

Girl. Woman. No matter what you are told or made to believe about yourself. Only you know how you truly feel. Be honest with yourself. If you are not getting what you want from a relationship or having any less positive feelings about yourself. Run. No, sprint. You truly deep down know how you feel and I promise you are more than worthy and as Marisa Peer says so beautifully, 'you are enough'. I just know you are. No one can argue with how you feel. They are not in your lovely, creative mind. Only you are. Be kind to yourself. I never felt love or worthiness when I got into that situation when I was eighteen. However, like I said before I do not blame this experience or person. I am thankful to him. It has made me who I am. Yesterday I got set free and my gosh I flew. I want you to fly with me. I want the exact same for you. No matter what life throws at you there is always a way to turn it into a positive. Be yourself. Be honest. Smile. Let's get started my lovely reader. There is unwavering 'hope' for you, girl. 'When life makes waves, enjoy the ride'. Queen surf those waves.

My aim for this playlist is for you to believe in yourself. Give yourself self-love. You are amazing. Exactly as you are. You are unique. I have a question. What truly makes you feel good? What is it that you think of and you instantly smile? It may be a person. It might be an experience. It could be a song. You are a powerful DJ and whatever it is that makes you smile, I promise you now there is a reason for it. It is as simple as that. Keep thinking of that image. For me, it is as you know my family and my friends, they make me happy. Yes, I did meet someone who was able to snap me out of any negative thought or feeling into a positive. Although this changed when I finished this magical adventure. I realised it was never him, it was me that was making myself feel good. I was sprinkling 'self-love' over me.

I took my first no-makeup selfie on the 29th January. I realised it was two days after I started this adventure. It is you my inspiring stunning reader that I want to thank the most. It is because of you, the young woman of today that we are reaching this beautiful destination of self-love and discovery. We did this ourselves. A lot of inspiration from both men and women along the way. Men and women can be a team, can't they? I would not be Ells without the men in my life. It is us that has made this happen. We are magical.

As you know when this started, I said to you I wanted to be as honest as possible with you. I knew that honesty would get us to that destination of self-love even quicker. When I wrote this book I asked the Universe if it could happen really quickly. I wrote the first draft of this book in 21 days. Twenty-one. The age I fell ill. Anything is possible, my darling Queen. You just need to believe in yourself. I did.

I want you to have this 'gift' a lot sooner than I did. I am so grateful for my past because honestly, it meant that I could share it with you and assure you that life does not make sense sometimes, let's be honest. Whatever it is you are going through, social pressures maybe, any less positive experiences. I promise you, it will make you the strong, unique, special person you are and it will all make sense one day. You will wake up one day and that 'missing part of the puzzle' will be there staring you in the face. I did not finish my degree. My title was about women in modern day society. The idea of being 'perfect', I could not get my head around it. I now look back and it is because there is no such thing as 'perfect'. The songs 'Who You Are' - Jessie J and 'Perfect To Me' - Anne Marie come to mind. Two stunning songs that I believe are made for us. They are the future for female thinking, right?

Looks like we need to start thinking and feeling. Your imagination is your 'pal'. Your best friend. For years, I did not like what looked back at me in the mirror. Even at my lowest weight I saw someone less attractive than the woman I see now. After sessions of therapy, reading incredible books and listening to lovely podcasts in particular listening to the wonderful words of Tommy Gentleman, I started to believe in myself and my 'message' and dream. Life-changing speakers have contributed to helping me 'roar'.

I now know how to cope with challenges through awareness of who I am. I want the same for you. I have spoken about a few people who have contributed to this, if you want to look these lovely people up, then do. Another one is Vex King 'Good vibes, good life'. I knew when I read that I was ready to live a 'good vibe' life. This is all thanks to that trip I made to Hay House in London. I woke up one day and I said I am going to who I believe to be the best publisher in the world. I did it. I bought them lion bars because I wanted them to hear me Roar. I was recommended this book, so I called three different Waterstones near to their location. One shop had it so I reserved it and jumped on the next train to go get it. That is the kind of chasing I will now do. Chasing my dream. I want this for you too. Chasing a dream is far better and rewarding then chasing the wrong kind of butterfly who ultimately is not meant for you.

I want you to have a look in the mirror now. If you do not have an opportunity to do this right now then you can give it a go next time you pass a mirror. I will do the same. What is the first thing you see in that reflection? For me, it is my red cheeks. I used to have red cheeks growing up and I always related it to being overweight. I now look in the mirror and I am saying 'your body is perfect'. I truly believe it is. I know this exercise may seem difficult but I believe in you.

Look at yourself and say 'I am' before three positive words to describe your lovely self. It may be your hair. Feel how lovely your hair is. It may be your eyes. See how beautiful your eyes are and say 'I am' and the first positive word that comes to your mind. Only positive words to be used. I have a feeling your smile appears in the top three. If it doesn't, then I'm sure there is something even more special for you to appreciate about yourself. I want you to say 'I am beautiful' after spotting your favourite attributes of yourself. The best way to really feel that love for yourself is thanking these qualities because giving thanks to something honestly makes you feel more warmth to your lovely heart. The more gratitude, the more positive the attitude. Own it, sister.

Remember the people in your life who make you feel good about yourself. For you, it may have been a friend in your life, a relative or even a neighbour. Maybe a boyfriend. Whoever that person was that made you feel good at that moment in time, thank them. Smile when you thank them. It is not them that is making you feel good, it is you. Remember that song from the introduction. Play it. Think of it. Feel that beat. I heard this song in September 2018 when I started seeing my therapist. I loved the song. My body would move in ways it has never moved before. This song was the one I played the day I said to my mum she could record a video of me dancing to it on the

24th January 2019. Something I have never done for her, since I was a young cub. The day I started a gratitude exercise on love. Little did I know then three days later I started this magical adventure with you, reaching, I can't believe I am saying this real 'self-love.' Hello self-love, we love you!

I am watching the video now. It was made for my mum. I wanted to show her I knew. I just knew life was about to transform into 'magic'. I knew that dance for her made her believe that I had found my purpose. I found my purpose with you. Do you like to dance? I bet you can dance. Even if it is just a little hand wave or a little twitch in that lovely foot of yours I bet you can dance. Even if it is just imagining it. You can dance. Your mind has visualised it so it is possible. You are possible. Whichever song you chose at the start of this adventure. Have a little dance if you want to. Or even a sing. I can assure you whatever, whoever makes you feel good. Remember them. They are cool but actually you are even better. Be natural and be true to yourself. You can achieve self-belief and therefore reach self-love. Do you remember at the beginning of this journey I told you about a 'gift' you have. I have a little feeling we are about to find out yours.

When I listen to 'Body' by Loud Luxury I feel good. Music can be interpreted so differently by everyone. I do know that I love the beat of this song. Experiences with men taught me that a man would not make me happy, I would make myself happy first. Things are very much about to change. I am ready for real love. Truth. If worse comes to worst, as Ariana Grande says so beautifully in her song 'Thank you, next'. 'Least this song is a smash'. As is this book, it has been created through you and I, Queen. We have reached a large sprinkle of self-love. Similar to Ariana's lyrics, we turned out 'amazing'. Especially you, woman.

'Never give up on what you really want to do.' Thank you Albert Einstein! So that gift we spoke about of yours, I wonder if you know what it is. What do you enjoy doing? It is quite a general question but I think simplicity is good here. What makes you feel good when do you do it? It may be a sport. It may be a talent of singing or dancing. It may be walking your dogs. You may love animals. It may be helping people. It could be technology related. It may be involving a 'team-like' environment with your family or friends. It could even be public speaking. It could be your favourite subject at school that you enjoy doing. I did English, Psychology and Religious Studies/Philosophy at school. I never thought about this until now but I loved these subjects. Genuinely, English was super fun, I had the funniest class. The individuals that made up this class were great. Mr King comes to mind because he was my English teacher at school. I remember a lot of giggles in his class. Psychology was great for me. A very interesting bunch with a lot of my good friends in my class. Then religious studies/philosophy. That was my favourite. I was surrounded by cool people. Every teacher and classmate in these subjects inspired me, even if I didn't show this at the time.

Exams can be tough, of course, but look out for those people that make you smile in those lessons. Learn from them. Learn from your teachers if you find them positive and supportive. Education is great. There is a reason you have chosen those subjects. Stick to them if you enjoy them. Whatever reason it is you chose them, I am sure you will discover why in later life. If you didn't do GCSE's or A-levels, there is always an opportunity to do them. Although, if you have not done them, I'm sure there is a definite reason why you haven't and I bet you know deep down why and what you will achieve from not having this experience. If you did want to do them, ask someone who can give you good advice on what steps you would need to take to achieve this. Maybe even a friend, relative, or charity.

Remember the guy I told you about in this adventure. The 'everytime' one with reference to Ariana Grande's beautiful song. We used to have a lot of banter with each other. We would be quite critical of each other. I look back and he once said to me 'you're not very clever are you?' I tried to throw banter back but actually it didn't make me feel great. I remember saying to him, 'ummm I have a degree!'. Even if I hadn't passed it, I wanted to try and 'banter' him back. Be true to yourself and know your worth. Do not rely on other people to give you feelings of worth. Everyone has worth. That is what makes you so unique and special. Whatever it is that makes you happy, do it. You will be good at it. There can be restrictions or challenges you may face that could hold you back on reaching it quickly. However, I believe 'patience is power' I found this quote on Google/Pinterest recently. You can do anything you want to if you believe the end result will benefit you. Sprinkle some self-love on it. Listen to that lovely gut of yours we spoke about before. Connect that inspiring mind of yours to how you are feeling in your heart. Throw in a huge amount of gratitude and voila! Self-belief at your service. We should totally start a club. A 'cub club.' Just saying.

A friend of mine and I last week did something cool. We did this 'exercise' she found in a book that said to discover your core values. It said to write them down and do it with someone else. Then you both write down which values from a list that you think your friend has chosen for herself and for you. It was fun and easy to do. You should totally try it with a friend. The ones I wrote about myself were 'honesty, gratitude, kindness, empathy, spirituality, loyalty, adventure and success'. I hope I have brought this to the table in this adventure with you woman. The ones she chose about me were adventure, trust, truth, appreciation, respect, growth, peace/wild (she added wild in) and kindness. What a lovely choice. I thank her a lot for this. This friend in particular, I hope she knows that I never went anywhere even if she does believe I did.

Girl. Let's create **your playlist**. What music did you grow up listening to? Whatever genre it was, you were drawn to it for a reason. Listen to those artists that make you feel good. You chose those songs because of what they mean to you. Your playlist has been created by your thoughts and feelings. You, thought and felt a certain way at some point in your life and therefore selected that song or artist and added it to your experience and playlist. Through this magical adventure you have gained what I believe to be bravery, honesty, strength, independence, royalty.

You have set me free, so I hope you can apply this to your life and last but not least you have reached, a stunning appreciation of self-love. All the key parts of you that make you who you are. Which enables you to understand what you want out of life at your age. **Your thoughts are a playlist.** My once little lioness cub, you are about to become a Lioness in charge of the jungle, my friend. You ready? You know that you were born ready. This is coming from as you know a lioness cub who went pretty mute for about six or seven years. I am now sitting here in a lovely yellow top that I never believed I could ever 'pull off' or wear with confidence. I am happy. I am running off not a lot of sleep. Your playlist has energised me hugely.

I am going to take a selfie for you. Not thirty and delete them because I want this moment to feel real. I will do it in a second. Before

I go, there is something we should do. We need to flipping 'roar' don't we? Together. I have just put 'Together' on by Ella Eyre. This is the song I now imagine you and I dancing and roaring to. If this does not feel natural to do this by yourself, grab a friend. Grab a family neighbour or even a boyfriend. I will be doing it in front of my mirror. I will take the picture after I have 'roared'. I'd love if you did the same. It may be a picture, it may be a video, or even a voice recording. I am going to do a voice recording also. Whatever it is I want you to remember this moment forever. I know I will. The moment we 'roared' and began loving life as true lionesses. The moment we put ourselves first. The moment we said 'nah'. No if we do not want to do something that will affect how we truly feel about our lovely selves. I'm going to put the song 'Body' on by Loud Luxury when I do this.

If I'm honest girl, I did the recording as well and I burst out laughing. It was so fun! I couldn't actually believe what I was doing. I reverse that thinking. I believe it. I did it. You can do it too. I believe in you, my friend! I did take a picture and admittedly deleted it because I was covering my face because I was laughing so much! Girl, I want this to be fun for you. I did chill out for a millisecond and took one. One photo. I really hope you do see this selfie I took for you one day. I wrote down an affirmation last night about myself. 'I am a strong sunshine once girl, now woman. Thank you'. I have never felt so real and more like that Sunshine girl that was adored when she was younger. You have made this happen girl and I want this for you too. See yourself as a Sunshine girl because you are one if you believe it. Imagine it and it is there. I hope you have enjoyed this adventure as much as I have. I have a feeling you have. We have done this together. You and I. I want you to write an affirmation down as well before we finish this journey of self-discovery. It is your affirmation. Key word being 'your'. Your own one. Keep it to remind yourself of how stunning your mind and heart really are. They have made you, you. This adventure is coming to a natural end now, don't you agree? Be the lioness in your story. Create your own story and playlist you special thing.

'Beware; for I am fearless and therefore powerful'. - Mary Shelley

Beware world! There are Queen Lioness(s) entering the world and they are not afraid to roar! Hehe.

You and I both. Girl. Woman. You are enough exactly as you are.

Thank you to Marisa Peer and Louise Hay for inspiring the last part of this magical adventure. Both incredible women. Do not be afraid to be a woman. Be you. As you know I do not say 'goodbyes'. It is 'see ya' I hope that is okay with you. It is 'see ya' for now. However, I do have a little sparkly feeling we will be connecting again. Just a feeling I have. A 'vibe'. It may be through a word, or a picture, an event, even a book. It may be a lion poster you walk by. It may be a song. I promise you this girl, tiny lionesses roar the absolute loudest. That Lioness who once was quieter than she really was is you. You can roar. Ready to go see the 'wonderful world' that Louis Armstrong sings about? Ready? Shall we go see it for the beauty that is really there? I believe it, so I am going to do it. Shall we? Let's take a walk on the wild side!

'Hold up' (Beyonce song). 'Train noise' pending. Our train has reached that destination now. The destination of self-discovery and self-love. Hello you. Anyway, I need to go see to Simba! And so the magical adventure actually begins.

Go girl. The world is waiting at the edge of their seat ready to greet you at the 'Arrivals' lounge. They want to see your radiant smile.

Sending you a huge sunshine hug, 'your sister from another mister'. Big love and a huge sunshine hug. I cannot wait to hear you ROAR like the true Lionness Queen you are.

Your Sunshine Pal,

Eloisa x

P.S. 'I think I'm onto something, I feel the good times coming!' Ella Eyre you are ace. We feel the good times coming don't we Queen. See-ya. Soon.

Putting Playlist 8 Into Practice

The teaching of this final chapter is for you to feel like the survivor of your own story. I've said mine - now it's your turn.

I hope you always roar Queen. I never did and I will now roar for as long as I am here. You own your body, no one else. It is your choice what you do with it. I am grateful I have got to a place now where I am supported by incredible people that I can speak about how I was with men and not feel embarassed. I reached this through loving myself first. Be honest with yourself then a better life will appear. I am currently listening to 'Bad guy' by Billie Eilish as I write this.

On that note, do you remember the song I wrote about in your playlist? 'Hope' - The ChainSmokers is playing now and my gosh I have never felt so real and in touch with this world Queen. Say no. There is hope. We just need to believe in ourselves enough that we deserve the absolute best. There is a Lion or Lioness out there for everyone. We just need to believe in the magic of life and what it has in store for us.

Have self-love. Have self-respectt. Say no. The world can be your oyster. Follow your dreams. Believe in them. Visualise them. PAINT THEM!

I think it's time for a Sunshine selfie! Go post your own #sunshineselfie #TheSunshineAdventure @eloisaroars

Seven Day Affirmations to be said every day of the week for twenty days or more:

Monday: 'I approve of myself' - Louise Hay

Tuesday: 'I am Enough' - Marissa Peer

Wednesday: 'I am a strong Woman'

Thursday: 'I am an Artist'

Friday: 'I am a Queen'

Saturday: 'I am Beautiful'

Sunday: 'I am a Lioness'

A Sonnet

Do you ever feel like a robot
With a head full of butterflies
And a tummy full of knots?
Do you ever feel tears in your eyes
And wonder how a Lion roars?
Is the world too loud?
Do you wish for a pause?
Get some space from the crowd
and step inside,
Put your music on,
You have nothing to hide,
So sing your song!
I know sometimes it's hard and sometimes it's tough
But happiness is yours...because you are enough!!!

#TheSunshineAdventure

ABOUT THE AUTHOR

Eloisa is a twenty-seven-year old woman who has had years of mental health related personal experiences. She had her first panic attack when she was 16 years old when she lost her Dear Grandad. This translated into several illnesses aged 21 upwards. Six years of ill health and several hospital admissions led her to full recovery and positivity. This book started the day she connected with her grandad, who she realised was actually always there guiding her. From ill health Eloisa has flipped the once thought of as a 'negative' experience into the most positive, uplifting, 'contagious' (Virginia Morrell) 'blessing' (Rhonda Byrne') expression of self love that she wants to give to young women searching for self worth and appreciation. She wants to 'shine a light on anxiety' (Virginia Morrell). Eloisa wants this for the lioness, the young women of today, because she did not have this when she was young and ultimately led to years of self destruction. Eloisa wants young women to mindfully choose freely how they want to paint their magical picture of life. Through self belief.

CPSIA information can be obtained
at www.ICGtesting.com
Printed in the USA
BVHW031744270619
552132BV00001B/76/P